Meditations for Healing

Larry Moen

Published by: United States Publishing
3485 Mercantile Avenue
Naples, Florida 33942

Cover Art: Charles Frizzell © "Ethereal Journey"

Illustrations: Patty Smith

Printed in the United States of America.

Library of Congress Cataloging-in-Publication Data

Meditations for Healing/ [edited by] Larry Moen
p. cm.
Rev. ed. of: Guided imagery, v. 2.
ISBN 1-880698-69-2 : $11.95
1. Meditation. 2. Imagery (Psychology) 3. Visualization.
4. Self-actualization (Psychology) I. Moen, Larry, 1948-.
II. Guided imagery.
BF637.M4G85 1994
153.3'2 — dc20 93-34926
CIP

To Mom and Pop

Live in the heart,
and heal with love.

– L.M.

Contents

Introduction

To be healed implies physical and mental strength and freedom from disease. The dis-ease we encumber in our own being is a result of past programming. It has been my experience that this past programming can be purified through the process of guided meditation. For that reason, I have assembled this collection of healing meditations from a varied group of guides including psychologists, therapists, physicians, and others who offer imagery techniques as part of their lives or careers.

Each imagery can be perceived as a prayer. You are simply asking for and receiving what your umlimited Higher Self has to offer. Images can produce powerful emotions and unlock psychological blocks. As you turn inward, you may find Light, Truth, and Love, which may be different from your normal conscious state. You may also discover Darkness, Deceit, and Fear, which in this world of duality is only a mask covering the Higher States of Consciousness.

Love is a powerful healer that can be revealed or enhanced

through meditation. Creating a loving atmosphere is beneficial to those who are physically ill. Imagery can also help the body boost its immune system, increase the production of chemicals that encourage healing, and generally relax and promote the peace and love an individual needs to aid in the healing process.

Allowing yourself to love yourself has surprising consequences. It helps you become free, break down psychological walls, be fearless, and be strong. It is only after you love yourself that you can begin to heal.

Visualization has also been found to enhance learning, build self-confidence, and improve athletic ability. It is not magic and it is not supernatural. Guided imagery is a simple matter of relaxing, uncluttering your mind, and focusing your thoughts clearly on what you wish to accomplish. It helps create a more receptive environment to help you achieve your desired results.

During my many years of practicing meditation and unlocking the secrets of my own psyche, I have found that what we concentrate on, we receive. If a person concentrates on "not getting" negative results, negative results still occur because the focus is on the negative. On the other hand by focusing on the positive, one will move in that direction, receiving positive results. This book is filled with positive.

Another important healing benefit of meditation is the release of stress. When stress is not released, it can be internalized and cause psychological and physical damage.

Guided meditation is one of the many tools available for teaching people how to let go of tension, anger, fear, anxiety, and other stress-producing emotions that cause illness.

This book will help you change and improve your life by guiding you to your own Inner Strength. Such Strength is innate in each one of us, and while many people rely on outside influences, persons, or materials to achieve changes and growth, all the tools you need are present within you. Guided imagery helps you see yourself the way you wish to be. As you practice visualization, you become more and more comfortable with a new reality for yourself.

For example, if you are hesitant about speaking in front of an audience, you can visualize successful speeches and see yourself in front of an audience in a calm, controlled manner. Of course, you still must actually practice speaking in addition to the imagery. But the imagery will enhance your progress and success.

These meditations are given to you with Sincere Love and Hope that they will help enhance your personal abilities and mental powers. Allow yourself to let go and enjoy these experiences. You are all the things you want to be. Guided imagery will help you discover that.

– L.M.
February 1994

How to Use This Book

If you have never practiced guided imagery or meditation, do not be concerned. Everyone has visualized to some degree, and this book offers a variety of guided imageries that can be practiced by anyone following a few simple instructions. No special classes or courses are needed. If prayer is part of your life, then you have already experienced a kind of meditation. So relax and enjoy the journey.

Types of Meditation

While traditional meditation requires a quiet unoccupied mind, guided imagery creates a scene or group of scenes developed to fulfill the purpose of the imagery. An imagery designed to help you get ahead in your career might involve climbing a mountain or finding your way on a difficult jungle path. The object of the journey is to help psychologically orient yourself for achievement, healing, relaxation, or numerous other areas of change or growth.

Where and When Should I Meditate?

These journeys can be experienced by reading them silently or out loud alone or with a partner. You may wish to tape record journeys in your own voice and play them back at times best for you. You may also wish to share these journeys with a group.

Visualization can really be done anywhere. While waiting in a doctor's office, on an airplane, during a walk, or even sitting at your desk.

However, these journeys are best practiced in a quiet place where you will not be interrupted and where you can be in a relaxed position: with eyes closed lying down, sitting in a chair, or perhaps sitting in a cross-legged manner with your back straight. Do not choose a position because you think you should; choose the one most comfortable for you.

The best time for using a guided imagery is what is best for you. Often people will use uplifting, invigorating journeys to start their days; soothing, tension relieving imageries for midday breaks; and relaxing, creative visualizations for evenings.

Group meditations are useful for promoting creativity in work projects and for encouraging people to pull together for business or community activities. An excitable, rambunctious group of children can be calmed down using imagery as well.

Pauses

Many journeys have one or more a "pauses." The length of time you take at these pauses will depend on your own experiences: it can be a few minutes or an hour. You may determine the length of the pause before you begin or during the journey.

What if I Fall Asleep?

Some people have such relaxing experiences that they believe they may have fallen asleep. Usually they have not. But to be sure, you can place one of your elbows in a upright position so that if you start to doze off, your arm will wake you up as it falls.

Music

Music can enhance the journeys, providing it is quiet and does not contain abrupt changes in tempo or pitch. The tape "Creative Imagineering" is pure ambient music, which can develop or increase visualization abilities. An order form is located at the back of this book for this and other tapes.

Breathing and Relaxation

All of the exercises contained in this book provide basic instructions for deep breathing at the beginning of each journey. Be aware that this breathing is not gasping or hyperventilation but deep, slow, controlled inhales and exhales. Most people breathe from their mid- or upper chests, but deep relaxing breath comes from "belly breathing." Inhale through your nose and expand your stomach. When you exhale, contract your stomach and gently force the air up through your lungs and out through your nose or mouth, whichever you prefer.

But What if I Can't Visualize?

Give yourself permission to visualize. Allow your mind to play and create and expand on what images you do see. Be patient with yourself. Say to yourself "If I could visualize something what would it look like."

Begin by practicing with objects that are familiar to you. Imagine a room in your home, your favorite vacation spot, or the picture of a loved one. Add movement and color to the image and allow your mind to be free and wander through the pictures you are creating. Practice this as you would anything else and soon you will be able to visualize fantastic, imaginary scenes that will stimulate and enhance your guided journeys.

Turn now to journeys in this book. Look through them and choose the ones that are best for you at this time. You may wish to begin by reading them silently to yourself, then aloud.

Enjoy these journeys, their wonderful vivid images, their life-enhancing qualities, and their ability to help you achieve your goals and desires.

Healing

1

Affirmations to Awaken the Healer

Guide: Michael K. Wilson

Morning
I awake this morning to greater and deeper expressions of self-love.
I am totally at peace "within."
I allow the healing power of self-love to create health, wealth, and happiness in my life now.
Love heals. I am love. I am healed.

Day
Today, I lovingly release all anger, guilt, and judgment that I have directed toward myself or toward others.
It is now safe for me to move past and beyond all negative and limited thinking and move into the healing power of unconditional love for myself and for others.

Evening
As I sleep tonight, I am bathed in the healing power of self-love.
I allow my thoughts to be free tonight as I become one with the infinite force "within."
I am all powerful, and I now use this power to heal all areas of my life.

2

Cool Your Headache

Guide: Jule Scotti Post, M.S.

"Tension headaches usually respond to overall relaxation."

Introduction

This relaxation can be used for different kinds of headaches. Tension headaches usually respond to overall relaxation and attention to the specific area that hurts. Migraine headaches respond frequently to changes in head and hand temperature. It has been found that patients who learn to warm their hands and cool their head and face develop more control over their migraine headaches. This may be due to changes induced in the vascular system. Frequent practice with this imagery is necessary before a person develops the skill to change head and hand temperature at will. Daily practice for two to three weeks is suggested.

Find a place to lie down where you can rest undisturbed for this relaxation time. Leave all thoughts of the world around you behind and bring your attention into yourself. If you are aware of your headache at this moment, let the painful sensations go by, and focus your attention on the process of relaxation.

The Journey

Begin by taking a few deep breaths, releasing tension and discomfort as you breathe out. Now be aware of all the different muscles throughout your body. As you breathe out release any tension in your muscles, and let them become heavier and heavier as you become more and more deeply relaxed. Let a blanket of warm relaxation spread over your body, and let yourself sink down into that quiet place inside yourself. Your body is feeling warm, heavy, and deeply relaxed. Your mind is becoming calm and peaceful. You are ready to begin your inner journey.

Begin by picturing yourself sitting in a hot-tub on the deck of a beautiful cabin in the mountains. It is a lovely spring day. The sky is blue and you have a breathtaking view across the valley and the surrounding mountains. You can see the snowy peaks of the mountains and their green tree-covered hillsides. There are pine trees around the cabin. The deck and hot-tub are surrounded by the cool deep shade. Pretty mountain flowers are growing around the deck. You enjoy their bright colors and you can smell their fragrance in the clean fresh mountain air. You can hear birds singing and the water bubbling and splashing in the hot-tub. Now feel the warm water all around your body, soothing and relaxing your muscles. Enjoy how wonderful it feels.

Now focus your attention on your hands. Feel a jet of warm water gently massaging them. Feel that warmth penetrating into your palms, through the back of your hands and into your thumbs and fingers. Your hands are becoming warmer and warmer as you become more and more deeply relaxed. As long as you are here in the hot-tub, allow your hands to become warmer and warmer, as you continue to sink deeper and deeper into relaxation.

Pause

Now as you rest your head comfortably on the side of the tub, see someone who cares about you coming over to offer you an ice-pack for your forehead. Feel this ice-pack now cooling your forehead. Feel the coolness spreading over the top of your head. Feel that coolness spreading down your face and under your chin. Gradually feel the whole of your head filling with comforting coolness, which relieves any pain and melts away any tension. Your head is becoming cooler and cooler, and soothing sensations replace any throbbing or pounding you may have felt.

Some headaches are caused by tension. This coolness dissolves any tension away, leaving all the muscles in your head and face feeling relaxed and comfortable. Some headaches are caused when blood vessels dilate too much and a larger than usual volume of blood is pumped through them. This coolness helps the blood vessels to constrict again to just the right size, to allow for normal, comfortable blood-flow to your head. Feel that coolness now and see your blood vessels constricting to create comfort and harmony, to relieve throbbing, to cool and soothe your head and face. Sometimes a headache may focus in one area — perhaps the back of your head near your neck, across your temples, or behind your eyes. Bring this healing coolness to any area where you still feel pain or discomfort. Feel it soothing, relaxing, and nurturing this area, so that your head now feels comfortable and pleasant. Let this coolness continue to flow around this area until the last traces of any unwanted sensations have completely dissolved away. There is no need to be aware of this area any more. You can just lie back in the hot-tub and enjoy the mountains.

Now as you look around you, remember that anytime you feel tension or discomfort beginning to create a headache, you can recall this scene and let relaxation spread through your body. If you like, you can imagine yourself becoming like a snow-capped mountain, your head cool, your body stable and peaceful, grounded and in harmony with nature all around you. You have the inner strength and ancient wisdom of the mountain deep within yourself. Mine these treasures, for your own healing. Share you inner wealth with others who need your love and caring. When you heal and grow you have more to give and more to live for each moment of the day.

Pause

Now it if is time for you to go to sleep let yourself drift off into peaceful dreams and enjoy a night of deep rest. If it is time to go on with your day, return now to your awake state of mind, feeling alert, refreshed, comforted and strengthened.

Jule Scotti Post, M.S. is a psychotherapist who uses biofeedback and deep relaxation in the treatment of stress and chronic pain in a medical clinic in Maryland. She has a masters degree in Counseling Psychology and has trained intensively in the use of guided imagery and music in therapy. She has worked in private practice as a psychotherapist for nine years and has practiced meditation for more than twenty years. Recently she has studied the principles of Chinese medicine and also brings this perspective to her treatment of pain.

3

Crystal Gazing for Healing

Guide: Mina Jo Sirovy, Ph.D.

"Interrupt your mundane thought patterns and connect with the 'Higher Self' within."

Introduction

Crystals are becoming well-known images of healing and of our relationship with our creator. This meditation provides a path to healing power within and reminds us of our own and God's support. It furnishes deep, powerful healing energy, and a relaxing feeling so that you can "let go." Try this meditation once a day for three weeks if you are manifesting a dis-ease in your body.

The Journey

As you sit down and relax, allow yourself to focus inside to your breathing. As you inhale and exhale, let there be an open end to each breath — a pause to let yourself just be. As the quiet seeps in, know that all of you is slowing down and relaxing. Any thoughts that come in are permitted to pass on by without being analyzed or attended.

As you ask for a gift, you find cradled in your hand, a crystal. This one is emerald green, and it represents a beautiful healing that is available to you. Feel the crystal growing warmer in your hands as you both begin to match vibrations, and exchange energy. The power within the healing green crystal is radiating out into all of your body — into your hands, up through your arms, into your shoulders, neck, and head. It is also running down through your chest, your solar plexus, your stomach, pelvic area and through both thighs, knees, calves, ankles, and feet. As the warmth expands into each body part, you relax deeper and deeper until you are completely comfortable and completely safe.

Pause

As you gaze with your inner eye, you easily journey into the crystal finding yourself inside of it. All around you are facets of the stone reflecting soft green light. You see yourself reflected in the mirrors on all sides, and your body is permeated with the healing light. It's like being underwater in a clear green pond. Shafts of light/energy are gently bombarding you. As you shift your gaze to see through the crystal walls you can see giant hands gently holding your crystal with you inside it. Can these be the hands of God? You accept and trust these hands to be loving and gentle and caressing. They only wish for your highest and best good.

Pause

You allow yourself just to rest comfortably in this healing sanctuary. You feel completely safe. This relaxing cradling is something you've always yearned for. There is unconditional love flowing into your being — and you are just "being" in this moment. At this point in time you affirm:

"I love and accept myself exactly the way I am. I let go and let God. I belong here in this peace. This is my holy space. I honor and cherish my Being in this moment."

As you slowly regain your outer senses, you realize it's time to return to the outside world. You bid a temporary good-bye to this safe haven and gently leave the crystal, easily transferring back into your own body. You fit into all your extremities like a glove and feel comfortably aware of your physical being. Soon you feel the warm crystal still resting in your own hands. You bless it and thank it for its healing powers within and without.

Pause

Gently allow yourself to return to a better physical world — one which is slightly veiled with a green tinge of relaxation and expansion. Know that you are healed and that you can go about this day sharing this feeling with all that you touch.

Dr. Mina Sirovy, who resides in Oceanside, California, is a marriage, child, family therapist with degrees in psychology from the University of California; a master's degree from United States International University; and a Ph.D. from The Professional School for Psychological Studies, where she was also a professor. Dr. Sirovy is a transpersonal psychotherapist who calls herself a "stretch" instead of a "shrink."

4

Divine Love and Healing

Guide: Angela Passidomo Trafford

"Experiencing the God within is the ultimate journey of healing."

Introduction

This is the expression of health, joy, and inner peace that exists as a choice in the heart of every human being. While working with a client who was experiencing lung cancer, I was inspired to assist her by guiding her through this creative imagery. It came about spontaneously, but the meditation has since helped many clients in the healing of serious illness. I suggest that this visualization be done daily during illness.

The Journey

Center yourself in the divine love of God. Allow your body to relax. Feel a beautiful flow of peace, starting at the top of your head, allow the muscles of your scalp to relax.

Allow a flow of peace to flow into your mind, giving you a sense of deep serenity, a sense of trust, and a beautiful sense of love.

Feel this beautiful love flow through your mind and allow your rational mind to be at peace and to relax in the warm nest of this beautiful love. All is in divine order in your life, in your heart, and in your world.

As you give your mind the command to relax, allow yourself to feel a deep sense of comfort from your inner discipline. You are making the choice to relax your mind and to flow into faith and belief. With this choice, you are changing your world. Right now. As you begin to slip deeply inside yourself, feel the beautiful flow of peace wash behind your eyes — honoring your eyes as your true vision, your true perception. Allow your eyes to be at peace and to relax. Feel the flow of relaxation going down into your facial muscles. Allow a deep feeling of peace to flow into your face and feel all these muscles soften, as you relax. You are flowing into the peace and comfort of God the deep source of comfort within yourself. You are choosing to journey within to find peace, love, and safety. As you realize that there is nothing to fear, that you are safe, you consciously allow the flow of peace and relaxation to flow down into your throat and allow all these muscles to relax as well. As it reaches the back of your neck, allow this sense of love and nurturing to flow through the back of your neck and into your shoulders, and feel your neck and shoulders relaxing. Allow all the cares and worries and burdens of the day — any burdens that you feel within your life — to slip easily away.

Visualize them slipping easily from your shoulders like an old cloak that falls to the floor. Now allow yourself to feel lighter, with a sense of freedom and divine peace.

Allow this beautiful sense of peace to flow into your arms and elbows and into your hands, as you deeply relax.

A very soothing sense of trust and relaxation flows down your spine as you love and nurture every muscle in your back. Then consciously allow the flow of peace and love to travel down your back, relaxing all the muscles in your back. You are beginning to feel very, very light now; you are a spirit of love and peace and joy as your body relaxes and all the stress and tension leaves you.

As you realize your true nature, as you come in contact with the divine source within, as you remember who you are, a feeling of power and strength and support for yourself begins to emerge within you. You allow this power to emerge simply by choosing love and faith and peace. As you feel this flow of peace flowing into your chest, you allow your lungs to relax. As a deep sense of love and nurturing flows through your lungs replacing any fear or tension in this area, you feel the love and nurturing flow into your heart. Any constriction or tension now leaves your heart. Your deep sense of faith and trust centers you and brings you inner peace. Feel the peace and love flow into your pancreas, your intestines and kidneys, your liver and colon, into your stomach and through all the organs of your body, and through all your bones. Every cell of your body is permeated with peace and love, and you take a deep breath and let it out. It is so magical and so wonderful just to relax into the deep source of being that is your true self. Feel the relaxation flow into your waist, and hips, your thighs and knees, your calves and ankles, and way down to the tips of your toes. You are filled with inner peace and love. You now consciously give over to God, any burdens or problems within your life and you let go to faith and belief and the knowledge that all is in divine order. All is being taken care of for you. You are flowing in the river of life, joyfully toward your highest good. As you relax and let the burdens be released to God, a deep sense of joy and inner peace permeates your being. You visualize the most glorious mountains. You see the snow glistening in the sunlight, the blue, the azure blue of the sky; you are on the highest mountain in a rarefied atmosphere where all is truth and beauty and love and peace. And this love and peace is WHO YOU ARE.

Any disease that you thought resided within you body was just a result of wrong thinking and negative blockages that you have now released to the Universe, call upon God for help through prayer and meditation, using the tools within you — your mind and your spirit — to heal your body. Your body is now healthy and strong and free of all illness. As a result of your healing journey, you have found a space within yourself — a space that is joyful and peaceful and filled with unconditional love. You are worthy; you are deserving of your own highest good. There is no need to procrastinate that good any longer; you are alive within the moment, feeling powerful and strong. You are full of love as a beautiful cup overflowing with love, peace, and joy. Your love is flowing to all the people in your life, and all the people who you meet upon your journey. You are deeply fulfilled with a deep sense of inner peace. You know that you are not alone. You know that there is nothing to fear, that you are safe, and that you are always journeying toward your highest good. You are learning how to interpret life's experiences and turn those experiences to your benefit. You are learning to wait in patience and trust until you understand more, until more information is revealed to you. You are learning to stop, and trust in faith and then to take the action necessary to make powerful choices in your life that reflect the love in yourself.

You feel good about yourself. You feel your spirit soaring in the highest reaches of the Universe. Soaring in love and peace and divine freedom, the freedom that comes from loving yourself. Your body reflects this freedom and love with vibrant health. You are very, very peaceful, very powerful, healthy, and strong. You are on your path in life, choosing courage and power and strength in every step that you take, knowing that help will always be there when you need it, and turning to inner guidance and wisdom when choices are difficult. You trust in God to help you, and you flow in the oneness of life in trust, letting go in peace and faith. Feel the beauty and the freedom of your spirit, the white light within you that flows through your body, healing all areas of your body, casting out fear, and filling you with the divine love and presence of God.

You may journey again to this beautiful space within yourself, to the divine light within. You may live in the divine light if you choose to do so. Feel yourself resting in the arms of God, and allow yourself to rest. And now as you are centered, with a sense of well being and inner peace, allow yourself to begin to surface into consciousness, with a power and strength that you will bring with you into your day-to-day life. Know that you are loved and honored; know that your life is affirming your inner peace. And when you feel comfortable, when you feel ready, you may open your eyes.

Through her own experiences with cancer, journey of self-realization, and spiritual transformation Angela Passidomo Trafford has developed the gift seeing into people to help them transform their lives, their health, and their way of living. She resides in Naples, Florida, where she teaches people how to live through the power of belief and love in her practice, Self-Healing.

5

Healing Stars

Guide: Larry Moen

"Cleanse your system with the energy of a million stars."

Introduction

Open mindedness to the information that may result from this imagery is important. You may wish not to condemn, criticize, judge, or analyze the information but to choose to absorb it and let it flow through the magnificent body in which your Soul is housed.

The Journey

Close your eyes. Inhale slowly and deeply, hold it... then let it out. Breathe in again, hold it... and as you exhale release any built up tension so that you are totally and completely relaxed in every part of your body.

Imagine a moonlit night with millions of stars. Focus on the brightest star that you see. The star sticks out as very special. All of a sudden the star bursts into a million pieces and comes showering over you very softly, and you feel comfort, warmth, and peace shine over you. At this time, feel the warmth from the pieces as they blanket around you.

Pause

Now visualize many small, bright, white stars breathing in through the bottom of your feet. These stars of healing come up through your legs in a rolling fashion, accumulating more and more stars up into your hips. Coming up through your abdomen, hundreds appear, traveling through your chest, shoulders, now through your arms, to your hands. Still entering through your feet thousands of soft, soothing, white, healing stars now filling your head. You give them permission to heal you, as they begin to fade into your body, which absorbs each and every one. You now focus your attention on your feet, where the process repeats itself.

The stars enter again in a swirling motion, coming up, through your feet, your legs are filled with hundreds of wonderful stars. They continue onward entering your pelvis, buttocks, back, chest, accumulating by the thousands. Continuing through your shoulders, arms and hands, back up through your arms, up your throat into your head.

This time before they fade away, you take the strongest of the stars, gather them in a ball located on the right side of your stomach area. Gather them all from your head, arms, and legs and send the ball on a reconnaissance mission to an area in your body in which you feel some pain or discomfort and that you would like healed. Let that area absorb hundreds of these stars in your willingness to heal that point of your body.

Now again on your own, visualize another grouping of stars entering from your feet filling your entire body.

Pause

Thousands of white, wonderful, healing, soothing, beams of light illuminate from your glowing, white stars. Gather the strongest again in your lower stomach area on the right side. Allow hundreds of strong healing stars to comprise your ball. Send them to the same place or possibly another place; let that spot absorb the strongest healing stars and let them fade into that area....

When you are ready open your eyes and find yourself back in total awareness. Congratulations to you for improving your health. Thank your lucky stars.

Larry Moen is the editor and driving force behind the Meditations *series. As a Vietnam veteran, Mr. Moen has been aware that significant emotional events can influence one's life. Mr. Moen discovered that past programming from childhood forward can be healed and transformed using the powers of guided meditation. Subsequently, Mr. Moen embarked on an intensive study of guided visualization which he incorporates in his work with T'ai Chi, yoga and self-hypnosis. He currently leads meditation groups and speaks at seminars.*

6

Key to Good Health

Guide: Bernie S. Siegel, M.D.

"A tool that will help you empower yourself."

Introduction

As time has gone by, we have seen how the mind and body significantly interact and in a sense, are one. It can be used in conjunction with all other supports, including the medical profession and your spiritual resources. And in many ways I think, these will help you to use all of your resources. So take the time to help heal yourself. You deserve it. You are a gift. So create a safe, comfortable place for yourself. You don't have to move to take a trip.

The Journey

Look up and let your eyes close gently. When you are ready let my voice go with you and direct you through this healing interval. We will find keys that help open the doors, that make life easier, that lead us to feelings of health. Sometimes it is a struggle to find that inner key and open the door. As with all searches, they begin inside oneself. In a very special place, in a very special class, in a very special school, the school of life. And see yourself going to the school of life, a beautiful building, and over the doors the sign the school of life and the key to health. You are not the only student willing to learn and so enter the class and when the teacher comes and hands you the curriculum take a look at what the teacher has given you. What are the topics? the chapters? the various keys? Because if you don't hit the right keys your life won't be harmonious. And go through the book and if there are some keys that you know will be difficult for you, ask the teacher for help and take a moment to go over the content of the course with your teacher or may be there is someone you would like to tutor you. You are entitled to some special time, some individual attention.

Take a moment to absorb the content of the course. I want you to picture what's going to happen. Graduation day is coming because you have been willing to do the work and I want you to see the goal that lies ahead, graduation day. Your cap and gown, your name is called. You see yourself walking up to the stage. How does that feel? All of the people in your life are there, applauding, cheering, and your teacher hands you a diploma and a key and when you return to your seat, unroll the diploma. And what does it say on it about what you have achieved and learned and what instructions are there about how to use the key to heath that you have been given. As a graduation gift, all the people in your life have given you a new car and a new house and your key is a master key because you have learned enough to receive it and it will start the car and unlock the house.

But first let's go out to your car. It's important that we begin to explore new roads and you are the driver and you will decide which way to go because only you know the right way and the right path and the right lanes and the right turns and by paying attention to what feels right, you will come to your house. And once again use the key to unlock the front door and explore the house. Are there things in it that need to be changed? repaired? healed? You are capable because what you will find in the basement is a strong box marked "Key to Health" and once again your key will open it and all the tools will be inside, tools that will allow you to maintain your health, to repair your body and keep the mind healthy. And in the box will be a list of some of the things that need to be worked on now, so take a look at the list and see what you may need to work on now with your new tools to maintain your health. And work on those things and make the changes and watch how it feels when you begin to work on the process and all of this is a process leading towards the product that you will be happy with.

And once you've done that, it's time to go through your mind and body just as you would go through a house — eliminating anything that's eating away at you the way you would eliminate a termite or a pest. And you don't need to use poison to eliminate pests. If you are healthy, you will resist them, and they will go elsewhere because they don't come to a home that is filled with joy and love and beauty. They know they can't survive there. They thrive on resentment and anger and stress and so as you go through the house and open the closets and cabinets, if you find any problems, addictions, throw them out. There is a garbage pick-up every week. Dump the garbage or put it in the disposal to eliminate it. And then on the shelf put love, acceptance, forgiveness, peace and know that the object of all of this work is not mechanical but an inner healing, one of love and forgiveness because there are times when your body is limited but your body does not represent the only key to your health.

Your state of mind and often the body respond as a by-product to a healed mind because the two are one and if you are like many of us occasionally things get lost, and if you lost the key, where would you find it? It's unlikely that it will be right out in the open and in the light. It is more likely that it would be in the darkness, so if you ever lose the key to your health, don't be afraid to turn towards the darkness and look into it because the key will be there, which will allow you once again to open your strong box and find new tools to deal with any problems that you may meet, and if you are ever searching in the dark, remember you can pick up a torch and light your way and illuminate the dark corners in the rooms. You have that ability. You don't have to call an electrician to light your own way. You are capable of doing it yourself, and it will be worthwhile to find a safe place to keep your key. Maybe within your treasure chest and before you leave the house go through it once again.

Are there any things that you've overlooked — rooms that you were afraid to enter? It's important to take a good look at your living room. Is it orderly? Is it comfortable for you to be in? If not, be the decorator. Make it your living room — a place that you can always come to and find peace and contentment and a state of well being. Perhaps a clock that chimes or sounds so that every hour you are reminded to be at peace and to think of your own health and wellness because you are a precious gift to yourself, and if you can love yourself, you will love others and if you love others, you will always be happy and always have people to love and always receive love.

And when you feel ready, come out of the house into the garden again, and you will see a beautiful fountain of health. As the water shoots up into the air and the sunlight goes through it, a beautiful rainbow will appear. Invite all your friends to form a circle of healing. Your friends, your family, people you know and work with, all of them. Bring them together in this circle and allow the love and the healing to spread around the circle and let the fountain of health bathe you, cleanse you and heal you. Let the warm healing waters wash over you and even through you. And let them eliminate any problems in your mind or body — physical or emotional all dissolve in this magical water from the fountain of health, and every time you take a drink of water you will remember this wonderful fountain of health and it will help you wash away all of your difficulties and restore your health.

And for all that you've done, there is one more gift for you. Walk forward and reach into the fountain. There is a gift beneath the surface that you can find and bring it out and learn from it and accept it and add it to your strong box and when all of your tools are safely put away and the key is in a safe place where you can always find it, take a deep breath of life and just let it radiate through you. Let every cell be open to life and health and love, and when you are full let that radiate beyond you to touch all the others and let their light and love touch yours and take that light and love and store it again in your treasure chest so that our light and love is with you and your light and love is with us. And if anything ever threatens your health, take the key to your health and open the chest and the strong box and that light and love will come to restore you and heal you and support you and light your path back to health.

And when you feel that happening inside you, allow yourself once again to return to an awareness of your mind and body, allow yourself to return, each breath making you feel more and more alert and more at peace until when you are ready you return by opening and becoming a new eye, an eye that is ready to proceed with whatever you would like to do at this time.

Bernie S. Siegel, M.D., attended Colgate University and Cornell University Medical College. His surgical training took place at Yale New Haven Hospital and the Children's Hospital of Pittsburgh. In 1988, after publishing his first book, the bestseller "Love, Medicine and Miracles," Bernie became president of the American Holistic Medical Association. His most recent book, "Peace, Love and Healing," has also become a bestseller. Bernie now travels extensively with his wife, Bobbie, undertaking a heavy schedule of speaking engagements and workshops, where he shares his ideas, techniques, and experiences regarding the roles of love and understanding in self-healing.

7

Magical Washline

Guide: Doris Hilpert

"Our psyche is a deep, wondrous, mysterious place, constantly creating, doing, and undoing."

Introduction

Creating a sense of peace and security is as important to fighting disease as medical supports. This meditation offers a clear imagery to reach the deeper layers of being. People have a tendency to bury uncomfortable feelings and emotions, and this visualization helps "unhook" the shadows we have created. It can free us to become more conscious, freer, happier, and more loving. Do not be rigid with meditation; visualize and create images according to your needs at a certain time. For the best benefits practice daily because life constantly creates, therefore it is good to be vigilant in how we respond.

The Journey

Sit comfortably in an upright position, feet firmly on the ground. Close your eyes. Take some deep relaxing breaths. Deep inhalation, slow exhalation. Deep inhalation, slow exhalation. Feel, how your breath becomes slower, deeper, more relaxed. Repeat these words several times: "Peace, be still, Peace be still." Feel it happening deep inside. "Peace, be still." Release all tension of the day. Whatever thoughts are wandering around in the mind, let them go. For this very moment relax from all fear, guilt, worry, tension, and doubt. This is your time for healing and inner reflection. When we heal the mind, we also heal the body.

Pause

Now, as you are fully relaxed, harmonious and peaceful, picture yourself in a very pleasant surroundings. It could be the healing sea shore, a green mature meadow full of fragrant wildflowers, or near a brook listening to the babbling sound of the water. Whatever wants to make itself manifest in your mind, get fully and deeply in touch with it. Feel the serenity of this very special place and how it has a wonderful healing effect on you. Feel, how your body harmonizes with your thoughts, feelings and emotions. Feel, how every part of your body becomes energized, revitalized.

Pause

As you are now deeply in touch with your innermost being, see, if there are still some disturbing emotions floating around, something which is in the way of harmony and peace. Where does it come from? How does it affect you?

Pause

Next to you, on two posts, you see a washline and underneath is a basket and some clothespins. Imagine that this basket is your unconscious self. If anything wants to come up that blocks your peace, take it out of the basket and with the clothespins hang it on the washline. See, how the gentle breeze blows it away. Wholeness and healing always go together. The more we know ourselves, our deep unconscious, the more we can reach this wonderful state. So — take your time in this clearing/cleansing process. Nobody is watching; it is just you and your deep feelings and emotions. The more honest you are, the freer you become.

Pause

Once you feel your inner soul cleaning is completed, slowly and gently come back to the present moment. Enjoy and celebrate your new freedom — and remember, the washline is always there for you, and so is the gentle breeze to blow away, your troubles.

In 1979, Doris Hilpert of Shelter Island Heights, New York, was diagnosed with ovarian cancer, stage III and was given several "death sentences" during the years. She practices intense healing and meditation/visualization daily, and according to her, "the doctors I come in contact with are amazed I am still alive."

8

Parkinson's

Guide: Janet Dean

"Using mind power helped me transcend the ravages of Parkinson's Disease."

Introduction

This visualization was created for a support group for those with Parkinson's Disease. I was aware of how much creative visualization helped me, and so I wrote this in an effort to show the group how they could use such imageries. It relaxes the body and mind. It is also important to learn to visualize, do positive affirmations, and create a healing atmosphere. I recommend soft music — classical, New Age, or religious — and I suggest this meditation be practiced in the morning and at night.

Energize the screen used in this imagery at least once a day, by thinking and creating it in your mind. Always see the solution to your problem and not your problem. Be careful to ask specifically for what you want and make sure you really want it. Put emotion into the picture, the wilder the better, and always see yourself in whatever scene that is playing.

The Journey

Sit comfortably. Close your eyes. If you have to change your position, feel free to do so. If your thoughts wander, bring them back to my voice. Take a deep breath and as you exhale, think "relax." Take another deep breath, exhale, and relax. Take a third deep breath and notice that your breathing has become slower and deeper. Continue to breathe, rhythmically and deeply. As I count from ten to one, your breathing continues to become slower and more even. Ten, nine, eight, relax and go deeper, seven, six, five, relax and go deeper, four, three, two, deeper, deeper, deeper, one. You are very relaxed and ready to relax even more.

Imagine you are standing at the bottom of a mountain on a path looking up at the top of the mountain, and you see a delightful, rustic cabin just the right size and shape for you. Now, start walking up the path toward the cabin. Notice how beautiful it is, the trees are extremely tall and shapely and all shades of green. There are flowers of all colors and varieties, some you've never seen before. The birds are singing and you pause to listen to them. How beautiful it is. The temperature is just right and the sun is warm. A cool breeze blows gently over your body and you feel happy and very comfortable. The little animals are very friendly. The rabbits, squirrels, raccoons, and some you can't identify come up to you and dance around you. As you watch them dance, a family of deer come up to you and the fawn licks your hand. At first, you are startled, but you see the mother and father smiling approvingly at you. You pat the fawn's head and continue along the path. The animals join you, and you all arrive at the front door of the cabin, which immediately swings open as if you're expected.

You pause and look in as the animals scurry past you and sit around the cabin. You see a big easy chair in your favorite color sitting in the middle of the room and you slowly walk toward it, sit down, lie back, close your eyes, and relax. A wave of relaxation starts at your head and moves down through your neck and into your shoulders, down through your arms and into your hands and fingers. Now the wave moves back up through your arms and into your chest, stomach, lungs, and heart. Down into your legs and toes, where it exits your body leaving your body relaxed. If you still feel tense, open your mouth a little. Sometimes just opening the mouth a little, will relax you.

Begin to create your own personal imagery. What is it you wish to change, heal, make better, or obtain in life. Think for a moment about the problem and decide what solution you want for your problem. Imagine a big movie screen on the wall in front of you. Remember you are viewing all this on the inside of your eyelids or in your mind's eye. After you have seen the problem on your movie screen, destroy the picture entirely. You can blow it up, break it up, tie it up or whatever will convince your mind the problem is over. Move that picture to the right and see the solution coming into the picture from the left. Do you want a healing? Then picture yourself healthy, see the doctor saying, "You've been healed." See yourself calling your friends and telling them, that you're healed. Plan on what you'll do now that you are healed and how you'll feel doing it. If you have pain, picture yourself free of pain. If you want to do something to change your life for the better, imagine yourself being complemented for whatever it is. If you want to obtain something, imagine yourself with the item or whatever it is.

It is now time to leave the cabin and come back to the here and now. Rise from the chair, the animals arise, too, and you all cross the room and the door opens. Turn once more and look around the room. Remember you can come back to this cabin at any time by just imagining it. You leave the cabin and discover the path down the mountain right in front of you. As you travel back down the path, you feel as if you're flying. The flowers and trees are just a beautiful as they were earlier, the birds are still singing, but you know there is a difference. You will always remember the experience you just had and it will become a part of your success. The sun is still warm and the breeze, just right. You get to the bottom of the mountain, and you sit down on a bench you find there. Before you leave, give yourself some positive affirmations. Silently repeat to yourself, "Every day, I'm getting better. Positive thoughts bring me the positive results I desire. I choose to be healthy. I know that good health is my natural state. I deserve good health."

It is now time to return to the here and now, right here and right now. I will count from one to five and when I reach the count of five, you will be wide awake and feeling fine. One, two, three, coming up slowly, four, at the count of five, you will be wide awake. Five, you are now wide awake, feeling fine, feeling better than before. Your eyesight it better, your hearing is better, and whatever problem you had is now solved. Welcome back.

Janet Dean has had Parkinson's for about ten years, but she keeps very busy, which helps her "keep the Parkinson's where it belongs — out of my thoughts." she says. She and her husband, Ken, are retired and reside in New Jersey where they host weekly spiritual meetings in their home.

9

Self-healing

Guide: Shdema Goodman, Ed. D.

"The possibility of erasing sickness from this planet is the main source of inspiration for this meditation."

Introduction

This guided imagery help to create health, harmony, peace, love, and joy in people's lives. I have experienced wonderful results in my health, and I have had similar comments from others practicing this technique. I recommend using this visualization at least twice a day—first thing in the morning and just before going to bed. The more often and the longer the better. At the least it is a great relaxation technique; any other results are bonus.

The Journey

Sit in a comfortable position. Close your eyes. Let all your breath become smooth and even — an equal amount of pressure throughout the inhale and exhale. Breathe in liquid love energy through the solar plexus (a bundle of nerve endings located above the waist). Slowly, softly, and tenderly send it into your left leg, nourishing and healing the billions of cells in that area. Fill up the right leg, the left arm, right arm; lower body; upper body; neck and head. Send extra dosages to the area that need healing. Visualize those areas already healed and perfect, shining and vibrating with health perfect. At the same time that you send the wet energy to that area. Use all five sense - feel it; touch it; smell it; taste it; hear the sounds inside; see its color and shape, see it perfect and filled with love energy. See yourself radiant, happy, peaceful, loving, lovable, flowing with health, as when all your life's goals are achieved. Send love and blessings to humanity and receive love and good wishes from humanity — open every cell to allow in the blessings.

Shdema Goodman, Ed.D., is a practicing psychologist in Livingston, New Jersey. She is an international lecturer and workshop leader and the author of two books "Babaji – Meeting With Truth" and "Come To Life."

10

Soft Belly

Guide: Stephen Levine

"Observing the relative openness or closedness of the belly gives insight into when and how we are holding to our pain."

Introduction

We are conditioned to suffer. The society of the hard-bellied and deeply pained conforms to this lowest denominator. We wander hard and lost through our lives until we awaken with a deep sigh of letting go and soften to the path of mercy.

When the belly is hard there is holding. Some degree of fighting or posturing is resisting and hardening to the moment, attempting to control. You may have to come back to soft belly dozens of times an hour.

The belly is an extraordinary diagnostic instrument. It displays the armoring of the heart as a tension in the belly. The deeper our relationship to the belly, the sooner we discover if we are holding in the mind or opening into the heart. Trying tightens the belly. Trying stimulates judgment. Hard belly is often judging belly. Even trying to understand what is being said now, the belly may tighten.

Don't try only to understand. Enter the process. In "Soft

Belly" simply allow understanding to arise, all by itself, from your true nature. Beyond the mind is everything you long to know. But the great irony of the spiritual search is that what we are looking for is what is doing the looking.

It is difficult to see that which sees, but not impossible. It takes some work to let go of old ways of seeing. Softening the belly is a beginning.

We are programmed to hold to our pain, to turn it into suffering. We are taught to harden the belly, to hide its fullness, its roundness, its spaciousness. Women in particular are programmed to be "attractive" and encouraged to wear undergarments that compress the belly and decrease the sense of spaciousness. Men, too, can often be noticed "holding in the belly" to be acceptable. We are implored to be hard-bellied by a culture which confuses hardness with beauty. It is a dangerous way to live if one wishes to be fully alive.

The Journey

Let your attention come into the body... Let awareness come to the level of sensation in the body... Feel the physical sensations of being in a body... Sensations of the buttocks on the chair or on a pillow... The pull of gravity... Sensations of the chest moving, the breath... Sensations in the neck, the weight of the head... Feel this body you sit in... Gradually allow your attention to come to the belly... And begin to soften the belly... Make room for the breath in the belly... Breathing in, belly rises... Breathing out, belly falls... Soften to receive the breath down into the belly... Allow the breath to breathe itself in soft belly.

Each breath softening, opening, releasing... Inhalation, belly rising, filling with softness... Exhalation, belly, falling, releasing any holding... Expanding and contracting belly... soft belly... The breath breathing itself in the softness... Letting go in the belly. Levels and levels of softness. So much grief held in the belly, so much fear and armoring. Let it all float in soft belly... Not hardening it to suffering... Just letting it be in mercy, in soft belly.

Notice how even a single thought can tense the belly, harden it to armoring, to separation, to grief. Letting go with each inhalation, softening the belly... Letting go with each exhalation, making space... Each exhalation breathing out the pain... Letting it go... Soft belly... Merciful belly... Levels and levels of softening... Levels and levels of letting go... So much room for liberation... So much room to be in soft belly.

Have mercy on you... Each breath softening... Softening the belly to uncover the heart... Letting go in the belly of the old holding that blocks the heart... Each exhalation letting go of the pain... Breathing out the hardness, the armoring... Making room for your life in soft belly.

Exception, judgment, doubt. Old griefs congregate in the belly. Softening allows them to disperse, to dissolve in soft belly. Pains, fears, doubts dissolving, dissolving into the softness, the spaciousness of a merciful belly.

Let it all float in soft belly... Have mercy... Levels and levels of softening meeting the moment... Levels and levels of being in soft belly... Breathing in, breathing out in soft belly.

Even if hardness is discovered in the midst of the increasing softness, just watch it float through... Let the hardness float in the softness... Nothing to change, no urgency in soft belly... Let urgency float in the softness... Room even for the pain in the mercy and awareness of soft belly.

Let the sound of these words pass right through you... don't hold anywhere... Trust the process... Let all that arises pass through the spaciousness of soft belly... And let your eyes gently open. And as your eyes open, notice at what point the belly tightens once again. At what point the "someoneness" reasserts itself and you feel a need to protect. At what point does armoring reestablish its long presence? Softening with the eyes wide open to the world. Practice softening to the pain we all share and the legacy of healing exposed in the deepening softness.

In the mid-1970's, while working with Ram Dass ("Grist for the Mill," 1976) Stephen Levine taught meditation in the California prison system. For the next few years he led workshops and learned from the terminally ill the need for deeper levels of healing and the profound joy of service ("A Gradual Awakening," 1979). In 1979 he began teaching workshops with his wife, Ondrea. As co-directors of the Hanuman Foundation Dying Project, as they continued to serve the terminally ill and those deeply affected by loss. Their guided Meditations for Healing grief, heavy emotional states, sexual abuse, and subtler forms of life/death preparation brought them international recognition ("Healing into Life and Death," 1987).

11

Unlimited Potential

Guide: Michael K. Wilson

"This meditation supports others in developing their own unlimited healing potential on the spiritual, mental, emotional, and physical levels."

Introduction

"Unlimited Potential" is designed to assist you in developing a greater awareness and understanding of your own healing abilities. I suggest that you read through the meditation once and then follow the steps as outlined. This journey is especially helpful for those with aids, cancer, or other life threatening illness.

The more you practice this healing meditation, the more open and receptive you will become to your own inner, unlimited, creative spiritual energy. With consistency and determination, you will achieve the positive results that you desire for permanent change in your life.

The Journey

Find a quiet place, and choose a very comfortable chair to sit in while you are holding these instructions in your hand. Focus your attention and your awareness on your breathing. Follow the breath as it comes into the body, fills up the lungs, pushes the chest out and then back out again. Make no attempt to control this process, just become aware of it. Now allow the breath to relax your mind and body. Release all stress and tension with each breath you take. As you become more relaxed and consciously aware of your own breathing, this awareness will awaken you to the power and energy of the life force that is in every breath you take and every thought you think.

Now once again follow the breath as it comes into the body, fills the lungs, and pushes the chest out and back out again. Close your eyes and for about two minutes follow the intake and outflow of your breath. When you feel you are ready, peaceful and relaxed, open your eyes and read this powerful healing meditation aloud to yourself with desire, belief, and expectancy. Begin to know and understand what you can conceive, visualize, and create in your own mind, will have the power and the energy to manifest in our life and in all your experiences.

I no longer dwell on what others think of me. I now understand that self-acceptance and self-approval begins "within." I now follow my own path with an open mind and clear conscience of what is right for me. I am now free from the past and all past experiences, and in this present moment, I lovingly acknowledge with unconditional self-love the divine unlimited potential of my being.

I know that my thoughts are the inner-creative power and energy that will build and create my outward reality. I am a miracle of love in action and in motion, and all I shall ever need will be provided. I now transcend all limited and negative thinking and dwell entirely on self-approval and self-acceptance in my life. I now lovingly express, with joy and happiness, the unlimited infinite source that has always dwelled within me as an individual.

Now for a few moments, once again follow with your awareness the intake and outflow of your breath. Notice the complete and total deep relaxation that has flooded your mind and body on all levels. With this awareness and the healing, relaxing energy in your consciousness; know that you have taken the journey inward and have aligned and connected with the healer within.

Michael K. Wilson is a writer and self-healing facilitator in Houston, Texas. His work is drawn from studies with people like Dr. Bernie Siegel, Louise L. Hay, Ann Wigmore, Shakti Gawain, Dr. Elizabeth Kubler-Ross, and others. He offers regular classes and is also available for lectures and private consultations.

Getting Well

12

Healing the Immune System

Guide: O. Carl Simonton, M.D.

"It's important for us to develop grounded, substantial beliefs that potentiate health and improve the quality of our lives. [We need] solid beliefs in our own natural healing mechanisms."

Introduction

Research has begun to show that within one's mind is a power to influence the course of cancer, and this is very exciting. It is clear and well-accepted that lifestyle influences health, sleep habits, diet, physical activity, job satisfaction, and relationships. Although the connection between these has been known for a long time, there is now known to be a direct link from the nervous system to the white blood cells. White blood cells produce nerve receptors on their surfaces, called neuroreceptors. A message can be transmitted instantaneously from the brain to the white blood cells, which are the body's basic defense mechanism. It is important to know the connection between emotions and white blood cells because white blood cells kill cancer.

In this guided imagery, you can learn to influence your emotions in a positive manner. This guided visualization is meant to provide you with relaxation and mental imagery techniques that will aid you in getting well. It is designed to work in support of your medical treatment, not instead of it.

So, I'd like you to listen and cooperate as much as your are comfortable - most of all take care of yourself.

The Journey

Begin by relaxing and getting into a comfortable position. If you have on glasses, you might remove them. Take a deep breath, and as you breathe out, mentally say "relax" to yourself. With every breath allow yourself to become a little more relaxed. As you relax, allow yourself to feel safe, comfortable, and protected. With every breath, allow yourself to become more relaxed and release any tension that you may be feeling in your jaw. You might open your jaw widely, and then let it relax. Let your breath send waves of relaxation all over your body. Relax the muscles of your face. Gently tell them to relax. Relax your neck, your shoulders, your arms, and your hands. Relax your chest and also the contents of your chest —your lungs and your heart. Let your stomach relax and all the organs of your abdominal cavity. Just let them relax. Let your pelvis, your legs, and your feet, relax. Think about being safe and comfortable and protected.

Feeling calm, appreciate what a pleasurable state your are in — how good it feels to be relaxed, safe, comfortable, and protected. Appreciate how these feelings — the feeling of safety, the feeling of comfort, the feeling of protection, the feeling of pleasure — are registered in your brain, in the old parts of your brain. These are very old parts of us, and as these feelings are registered, they stimulate an old portion of the brain known as the hypothalamus. The hypothalamus is the part of the brain that regulates most of the major systems of the body. Think about how these emotions influence your heart to beat more regularly, your breathing to be easy, your metabolism to be perfectly regulated. Allow yourself, as your body becomes more and more in harmony, to feel warmth spreading over your entire body. Everything is bathed by the wonderful, smooth workings of your balanced circulatory system. Now begin to imagine how these messages of calm, protection, comfort, and pleasure are transferred to your pituitary through direct nervous impulses *and* by chemicals that are released through your blood stream. Both stimulate the pituitary, which then releases its chemicals into the blood stream. These chemicals communicate harmony, calm, protection, comfort, and pleasure as they are secreted from your pituitary into your blood stream spreading throughout your body and coming in contact with one of the primary target organs: your adrenal glands.

Your adrenal glands, which sit in your abdominal cavity right on top of your kidneys, are getting messages of calm, protection, comfort, and pleasure. Imagine your adrenal glands responding to these messages and then producing their very potent hormones — their potent chemicals — which are released into your blood stream, and in turn regulate just the right pressure appropriate for calm, comfort, protection, and pleasure. Imagine the influence on your white blood cells as they receive the appropriate input from all these different sources of calm, comfort, protection, and pleasure. These waves of chemicals bathe every cell in your body with messages of calm, pleasure, protection, and comfort.

Imagine this happening throughout your entire body with great ease and with the naturalness with which it was intended. And now appreciate how these mechanisms have worked in us all our lifetimes, in the lifetimes of our parents, our grandparents, our great grandparents, and even our ancient ancestors before recorded history. Appreciate the intricate workings of your body and appreciate yourself for being involved in your own health.

Now begin to become more aware of the room you are in, the temperature, the amount of light, the sound. When you are ready, open your eyes and begin to appreciate how this works.

Imagine how fear would cause a very different reaction. The same systems and the same organs would be involved, but the reaction would be very different. Fear would be registered in different portions of your hypothalamus causing a firing of different portions of your hypothalamus, releasing different chemicals, and causing a very different message to be sent to the pituitary and very different chemicals to pour out of the pituitary. This would affect the target organs, the adrenal glands, very differently, causing a response appropriate to the emotion of fear. This would be a very different effect from the emotion of calm, comfort, and protection. And what if our fear is fear of our job, fear of our boss, fear of work, fear of life itself. What if these fears are bottled up in us, and we don't even know what they are? We can begin to see the incredible toll this takes on our bodies.

It is important to be understanding and patient with these mechanisms, which are subtle and intricate. It takes diligence to understand and apply these concepts that influence your health. The work is sometimes hard, sometimes easy. It can be very joyful even when it is very hard, and it is most rewarding, deeply rewarding — and deeply fulfilling.

13

Relaxing for Health

Guide: O. Carl Simonton, M.D.

"Relaxing on a regular basis and using your imagination to help shift your beliefs toward healthier beliefs... is important in terms of your health, your illness, and your life in general."

Introduction

Thoughts and emotions that are compatible with health influence our white blood cells directly through neurological pathways and indirectly throughout the hormonal systems. Healthy beliefs and healthy emotions influence them in a positive direction. It is important for cancer patients to know that when white blood cells are placed together with cancer cells, the white blood cells destroy the cancer cells. This is easily observable in a laboratory, and it happens in the body all the time. This meditation will help you appreciate the power and intelligence built into our white blood cells and to imagine them destroying the vulnerable, weak, confused cancer cells.

The Journey

Begin to take comfortable deep breaths, and as you breathe out, mentally say to yourself, "relax". When you are ready, let your eyes close and begin to feel safe, comfortable, and protected. Let the muscles of your face relax. An area that frequently holds tension is the jaw; so comfortably stretch your jaw open and then let it close to a comfortable position. As you do this, allow a wave of relaxation to spread over your body. With every breath become even more relaxed. Allow your neck, your scalp, and your back to relax. Let them relax. Breathe deeply, regularly, and comfortably, and with every breath out, mentally say to yourself "relax". Let your chest relax and your heart and your lungs. It can be helpful to think of a light shining out from the center of your chest — a wonderful light radiating out. Let the radiating light become a signal for your body to feel safe, comfortable, and protected. Relax your shoulders, your arms, and your hands. With every breath say to yourself, "relax". Let your abdomen relax and all the contents of your abdominal cavity, — your stomach, your liver, your intestines. Let your pelvis relax and your feet and your legs. Again, let your face relax. Relax your brain and all the blood vessels in your head, in your chest, and throughout your entire body. Let your whole body float in a wonderful state of relaxation, feel safe, comfortable, and protected.

Now prepare yourself to make the decision to get well. Remember how important it has been to make other decisions in your life. Recall the value of making decisions, and how you have decided and redecided important decisions in your life. Now deep in your heart and mind make the decision to get well in a way that feels comfortable to you. Appreciate that in doing what you need to do to get well, you will experience more of the richness and more the joys of life. You do not need to do things that will bring more pain into your life. The path to health is greater joy, greater love, and greater peace. Begin to think about your body's healing mechanisms, about how very strong, marvelous, intelligent they are. Know that the intelligence of your entire mechanism, your entire being, is communicated directly to your white blood cells. Your white blood cells — your body's healing mechanism, your healing energy — permeate every part of your being, flowing everywhere through your bones to the core of your being. Think about your white blood cells moving around taking care of anything that is wrong. Appreciate this, allow yourself to get excited about this.

Now think about the treatment you are receiving. Think of it as a friend, an ally, an aid to getting well. Appreciate the thoughts and efforts that have gone into this treatment; appreciate the mechanisms of how it works; and appreciate how the treatment helps you regain your health.

And now think about the cancer cells. Think about how weak, confused, and deformed they are, and how they are unable to repair even the tiniest damage done to them. Their only strength is their ability to multiply and divide. They never attack. Appreciate the weak, confused nature of the cancer cells, and the inappropriateness of them being where they are. Begin to imagine your white blood cells coming in and removing the cancer cells very easily, very automatically. As they approach and make the slightest of contact, they insert little tentacles of themselves into the cancer cells, injecting enzymes, and chemicals that cause the cancer cells to break up. This is done automatically. There is inherent wisdom in the white blood cells, and as the cancer cells break up, the debris is easily flushed through the circulatory system away from the area. It joins the larger circulation where the debris is filtered through the kidneys and liver and finally is flushed out of your system in your urine and stool.

Think about where the cancer is in your body, and if don't know or aren't sure, just relax your whole body and any area where the cancer is or might be. As the blood flow to that area increases, the oxygen level increases and the nutrients increase and the oncogene switches back to off. The cancer cells stop dividing and either die or revert back to normal cells, whichever is more appropriate.

Think about being more involved with life, moving in the direction of desire, passion, joy, and love. Think about more involvement in your work — rich meaningful work, whatever that means to you. Imagine being more involved with relationships — meaningful, important relationships. See those relationships moving in the direction that you want them to with more love and fulfillment. See your life becoming richer. See it as rich as it ever has been and more so. Get excited about life becoming richer than it ever has before. It will be different than it has before; appreciate that all this happens by moving in the direction of desire, joy, love, and fulfillment and away from pain, anguish, worry, and resentment.

Think about your life moving in the direction of joy, desire, and fulfillment and begin to bring that attitude into the room with you. Come back with a sense of peace. Become aware of the room, aware of the light, the amount of sound in the room, and anytime you are ready, open your eyes and prepare to go on about your day.

14
Visualizing a Health Plan

Guide: O. Carl Simonton, M.D.

"The results of patients' beliefs in their opportunities for recovery, coupled with their 're-decision' about the problems they face, are an approach to life that includes hope and anticipation."

Introduction

Our belief system is an important factor that influences our responses to difficult situations. The development of a two-year health plan gives us a structure on which to build the various aspects of healthful living. It helps us to develop those into a more harmonious lifestyle and belief system. This is a guide to be created with love and caring. It is not to be a harsh task-master. In order to help you facilitate this process, here is a meditative process integrating the two-year health plan into your life at an emotional level.

The Journey

Begin to get comfortable and to relax — breathing in and out. As you breathe out, mentally say to yourself, "relax". Release tension in your face and your shoulders; relax your chest and the contents of your chest — your heart, your lungs. With every breath, mentally say to yourself, "relax". Relax your abdomen and all the organs of your abdominal cavity. Relax your pelvis, your thighs, your legs and your feet. Relax your arms and your hands. As you become more and more relaxed, allow the feelings of safety, comfort, and protection to grow inside you. Feel more comfort, more safety, and more protection.

Begin to imagine your life moving in a more healthful direction and that the primary force directing this is your desire—a desire and passion for things in life, balanced with your inner wisdom that resides within and without. Sense your desire not just to do those things that feel good, but to do those things that feel good *and* are good for you. Directed by desire, using wisdom and using the structuring, develop your two-year health plan. Notice where you are putting most of your time and where you have most desire. What do you most want to do? Where is the greatest area of passion in your life? Do you get passionate about your role? Do you get passionate about your work?

If there is little or no passion, then begin to use your imagination to explore and see where the passion is hiding. Begin to bring it out of hiding and use your two-year health plan to develop it into a harmonious lifestyle for you. Where is the greatest amount of desire? As you think about life, where is the greatest amount of desire? Where is the least? Put little energy into areas where there is little desire. And put much energy where there is much desire. Allow yourself to grow, to grow wiser, using a gentle firmness, as you help move yourself in the direction of health. Relax. Relax.

Agree to be flexible as your desires change, as your passions change. Agree to allow yourself to gently shift focus, to shift your goals in life so that your two-year health plan becomes a loving guide and not a task-master. It is an instrument for you to use, not an instrument that uses you. Appreciate the wisdom that unfolds as you follow your desire and begin to creatively develop a plan for modifying your lifestyle so that you sail more smoothly and harmoniously through this sea we call life.

Pat yourself on the back for putting the time and energy into these exercises. It is a statement of your commitment to your health and your courage to explore these unknown areas. Pat yourself on the back and begin to become aware of the room that you are in, the amount of light in the room, and the various sounds, and anytime you are ready, open your eyes, and prepare to go about the activities of the day.

15

Inner Healer

Guide: O. Carl Simonton, M.D.

"[Some] patients have found that they can use their [inner] guide as a communication link to their unconscious, providing important information about their own psychological and physical workings."

Introduction

Our conscious intellect is only a small portion of the working of our body. So much of the wisdom of our body operates outside our conscious awareness. The more we are able to open to and understand this wisdom — the wisdom of the universe — the more we are able to live effectively; so having a method of doing this is of great value. Following is a meditative process that is one way of accessing this inner wisdom. It is a simple relaxation technique. In this meditation when we come to the point of addressing the wisdom that resides within and without, be aware that it is your own imagination. If you don't already have an image for this kind of higher wisdom, it's important for you to push your imagination and create a form for yourself. This is a way of pushing your beliefs, and allowing a framework in which change can happen.

The Journey

Get in a comfortable position. If you have on glasses, you

may want to remove them. Begin to let your eyes close and with every breath begin to feel more relaxed. Let the tension go from your mouth, jaw, and eyes and begin to feel safe, comfortable, and protected. Appreciate the many changes that occur in your nervous system and the different chemical substances being elaborated in your body as you respond to the feelings of safety, comfort, and protection. The blood flows through your body carrying these wonderful chemicals, and the nerve impulses going through your body signal calm, comfort, and protection. Let a nice relaxing, warm feeling spread over your entire body as the blood goes to every cell. It bathes all parts of your body with the nutrients and the balanced chemicals, which communicate messages of peace, calm, comfort, and protection. Let your chest relax and the contents of your chest — your heart and your lungs. Let your abdomen relax and all the organs of your abdominal cavity. Let your arms, your lets, and your pelvis relax and begin to appreciate the wisdom that resides within you and outside you.

This is the wisdom that lives throughout the universe; begin to appreciate the order, the beauty, the intricacy, and the perfection of the universe. Acknowledge that the universe wants you to be well, wants you to be healthy. The universe wants you to be healthy, happy, to be truly successful and fulfilled, and it will help you in achieving health, happiness, and the truest success and fulfillment. Appreciate that all of life is a loving teacher, with some lessons being easier and more desirable, and some lessons like cancer and life's problems being difficult and less desirable. Realize that all lessons are intended to bring you closer to who you are. Here you will be healthier, happier, more successful, more at peace, and have more wisdom than before.

Now in the quiet of your own being, address that wisdom that resides within and without in whatever form it manifests itself—a guide; a light; the form of someone you know, have known, or have read about; a special relative; a guardian angel who you've known from childhood; or an animal. Whatever form it takes is O.K., and if no form comes, create one using your imagination to move your beliefs in a desired direction. Gently use your imagination to form a source of this wisdom with which you are comfortable. Ask this source of information whatever it is that you want to know. What you need to do to get well. What you need to do to be more of who you are. No question is too large or too small. The connection with this source of wisdom gets stronger with use, and it is important to act on the information received. Ask whatever questions are important to you; ask whatever questions you want to ask, and then be still and let the answers be revealed.

One of the primary reasons we have difficulty receiving the answers is because we are not prepared to receive them. We are not willing to receive the answer, or we've asked the question in such a way that it's impossible to appropriately answer the question. So when there is difficulty in receiving an answer, return to asking the question with clarity, openness, and honesty, and an answer will come. It's important to be open to receive the answers in a variety of ways. Be open to the mystery of the workings of the universe and be open to the mystery of the wisdom of the universe. Generally, answers will come in a few days, if not immediately. The answers are there as soon as we ask the question. If the answers don't come soon, then ask why the answers aren't coming. Ask for clarity; ask for help. Relax and ask the universe for help. Open to the universe for help and imagine yourself well; imagine yourself involved in the healthful activities of life; imagine your relationships improving; imagine your work improving; imagine all things important in your life moving in the direction that you would like for them to go; imagine yourself living life with more excitement and more enthusiasm.

Begin to be aware of the room you are in, becoming aware of the amount of light and the sounds in the room, and anytime you are ready, let your eyes open and return with a sense of calm and peace.

Formally trained as a radiation oncologist, O. Carl Simonton, M.D., has pioneered an innovative approach to the psychosocial care of cancer patients for the past fifteen years. Through the use of visualization and meditation techniques, patients are encouraged to utilize their imagination to enhance their health, affecting changes in the way they view their treatments, quality of life and course of disease. He is co-author of two best-selling books, "Getting Well Again" and "Stress, Psychological Factors and Cancer." He is the founder of the Cancer Counseling and Research Center and the Simonton Cancer Center.

Relaxation & Stress Release

16

Constructive Rest

Guide: Pauline Fisher, B.S.M.A.

"Re-align your body in a 'non-doing' way."

Introduction

This technique is a variation of a method from Lulu Seveigard's book "Human Movement Potential." My interpretation of this work is another way to include body awareness with relaxation and quieting imageries. It is also especially helpful in relieving lower back stress.

The Journey

Before starting, take off or loosen anything that may be binding or uncomfortable such as jewelry, belts, or waistbands. Find a chair or couch where you can place your legs while you lie on the floor in a comfortable position with space around you and behind you. Place the backs of your knees on the edge of the chair, arms crossed over your chest and flop down, letting go of the arms. Do not hold them. Allow the fingers to fall to the floor or toward the floor. Close your eyes and take a few deep breaths, imagining your breath traveling from your toes to your legs and pelvis, your torso, arms, neck to the top of your head. As you exhale, feel the warmth traveling through your body and at the outer extremities of your fingers and your toes.

Take a deep breath, following the breath with your mind's eye through your body and out. Imagine your legs are on a hanger, like a pair of trousers hanging from the ceiling, your knees folded over this hanger, your legs totally relaxed as they are held up for you while your body remains laying on the floor. See all the creases of the trousers gently falling into the floor to the joints where your legs connect to your hips. Imagine tassels hanging down from the ankles. Imagine that the fronts and backs of these trousers, above the kneecaps are touching. As you inhale, feel all of the creases at this point in the trousers collecting, and as you exhale feel them falling to the floor. In your mind's eye, repeat this imagery. As you inhale, remember to collect the creases and as you exhale feel them falling to the floor. Repeat this once more. As you inhale, collect. As you exhale, feel the creases falling all the way to the floor at the joints that connect your legs to your torso.

Imagine that your are wearing a tuxedo jacket with tails and the tails of this jacket are laying on the floor under your chair. The jacket has a scoop neck and long-sleeves with tassels around the wrists with the arms still crossed over the chest. See these tassels falling toward the floor. Now imagine that someone's hands are gently pressing your rib cage on the front of this jacket, gently rocking you as you inhale. As you exhale, feel the front of the jacket touching the back of the jacket on the floor. Once more as you inhale, feel the hands gently rocking your torso from side to side, and as you exhale feel the jacket melting to the floor, the front of the jacket touching the back of the jacket on the floor.

Now imagine that you are wearing a turtleneck sweater under this jacket and feel the turtleneck extending above the scoop neck. Feel an imaginary hand lightly touching the area of your sternum, the center of your chest between your breasts. As you inhale, feel the front of the turtleneck expanding before it totally melts to the floor. As you exhale feel the front touching the back. Once more, inhale and as you exhale, feel the imaginary hand gently rocking your chest from side to side as the front of the turtleneck totally melts to the floor touching the back of the turtleneck. Imagine also that on your head you are wearing a funny little hat like the court jesters used to wear, made out of triangles that are connected and with tassels all the way around. As you inhale, see and feel that little hat, and as you exhale, feel it totally melting to the floor.

Imagine that there are a lot of creases at the base of your spine and at the top of your pelvis. Now imagine a pair of hands at this place and see the fingers collect all of these creases as you inhale, and as you exhale the fingers stretch all of these creases, all the way to the bottom of the jacket at the base of the tails. Once more in your mind's eye see those fingers collecting the creases as you inhale and as you exhale, feel them stretch all the way to the tails at the bottom of the jacket. When you are ready, once again imagine these fingers, this time a bit higher near your rib cage area and close to your spine. There are not as many creases in this area as there were near your pelvis, however, the fingers will collect what creases there are. As you inhale, feel the fingers collecting. As you exhale, feel them stretching all of these creases down to the bottom of the tails of the jacket. In your mind's eye repeat this once more, remembering, as you inhale, to feel the fingers collecting, and as you exhale to feel the creases stretching to bottom of the jacket.

When you are ready, this time imagine the fingers near your shoulder blades and again near your spine. Here again, there are not as many creases as there were in the other areas, but as you inhale, the fingers collect what creases there are, and as you exhale, the fingers stretch these creases all the way to the bottom of the tails of the jacket.

Once more in your mind's eye, inhale and collect and as you exhale, stretch the creases out, lengthening your spine. Now gently change the position of your arms, so that your elbows are on the floor and your fingers are lightly resting on your hips (or waist wherever it is comfortable for you), opening your shoulder blades a little and allowing your shoulders to drop.

Now imagine that there are a pair of fingers under you, near your spine, at the top near your shoulder, and in front near your clavicle, the bone under your neck. This time the fingers will be stretching the creases toward the walls on your side. Collect as you inhale and as you exhale, feel the creases stretching all the way past the shoulders all the way toward the walls, widening the jacket. Once again, feel the fingers in the back near your spine and in the front near the clavicle as you inhale, collect, and as you exhale, stretch all the way to the walls widening this jacket. Repeat this on the other side.

When you are ready, move these imaginary fingers near the rib cage area and near the spine. As you inhale collect the creases, and, as you exhale, feel them stretching out toward the walls from your sides. Once more, as you inhale, feel these fingers collecting the creases and as you exhale, feel them stretching all the way to the walls. Repeat this on the other side.

Now move these fingers down near the top of the pelvis. As you inhale collect the creases, and, as you exhale, stretch them out toward the sides of you. Once more with these imaginary fingers down near the pelvis inhale and collect, and as you exhale stretch beyond, beyond. Repeat this on the other side. Envision a pair of hands touching your sides. As you inhale feel these hands, and as you exhale feel the sides expanding. Once more, inhaling and feeling the hands and as you exhale feel them stretching toward the walls, along with the jacket and your body. Envision the base of your spine — the coccyx bone — and envision the top of your spine, feeling your spine extending all the way to the top of your head. As you inhale, be aware, as you exhale feel the two ends extending, stretching, and lengthening. Repeat once more with your awareness on the two end from the coccyx bone at the bottom of your spine to the top of your head. Now inhale and as you exhale, feel your body lengthening. Allow your thoughts to float, but do not be attached to any of them. Become aware of your body, its weight, and the feeling your legs hanging down. Very gently when you are ready, come back with no force, no rush. Bring your knees gently, to your chest and with as little tension as possible come to a sitting or standing position, maintaining the consciousness of your breath, your body and the feeling of relaxation.

Pauline Fisher, M.A., is a therapeutic movement educator and stress management consultant, as well as the author of a book. Her articles have been published here and abroad. She has been a recipient of many grants and is on the faculty of The University of Maryland. As the founder of A Moving Experience she does presentations and trainings throughout the United States and Canada. Her audiotape "Relaxation and Imagery" is available by writing to A Moving Experience, 1884 Columbia Rd. NW #105, Washington, D.C. 20009.

17

Enchanted Cove

Guide: Madeleine Cooper, L.C.S.W.

"Sometimes we need permission to lay down our burdens."

Introduction

The beach represents a relaxing, special place to many of my clients, and so this imagery was inspired by my own experiences in the coves along the central coast of California. It provides relief to chronic stress and an extended experience with peace. A severely anxious or depressed person is advised to start by using this imagery three times a day. Otherwise it can be used in the evenings.

The Journey

You are feeling comfortable and at ease with yourself as you continue breathing normally with your eyes closed.

Now you see yourself at the top of an open air staircase that leads to a beautiful beach. You look out towards the sea and before you are glistening waters. The sea breeze blows your hair and you breathe. It smells wonderfully clean. Let it caress you, the surface of your skin. The beach is inviting, so you grasp the wooden rail and start descending the sturdy hand-hewn steps.

As you go down the stairs, each step takes you into a deeper state of relaxation—deeper—deeper. Down the stairs—safe — safe — comfortable — deeply relaxed.

And now you are on the beach. The warm sand is beneath your feet. You take off your shoes and leave them at the bottom of the stairs. The sand feels warm beneath your feet. You sink into it, and it feels good as your toes curl into the tan giving grains. You take long strides eager to get to the shore... you are so relaxed... you feel so safe — strips of kelp — bits of abandoned driftwood — sea shells.

There you are now, where the water and dry beach meet. You walk along the edge of the shore.

The surf is pounding. On one side of you the waves rush in and little bubbly foam plays with your toes before rushing back to sea. You are so relaxed.... A sea gull flies above you and calls. You follow it, and suddenly you find a cluster of moss-laden rocks. You climb easily over them. You find yourself in a small, quiet cove.

You look around at the wonder of it. The cove is shaped like a horseshoe. You still see the ocean dappled with sunshine and small, white crests. There is a ship passing in the distance. You deeply breathe the moist salt air and smell the oceans fragrance. The gull has flown away leaving you in this special chamber... your own private beach safe from all the world. The sound of the surf that pounded before, is muted.

At one end of the horseshoe, which is formed of golden sandstone and clusters of dark rough rock, your eyes light upon a shelf. You go over to it, and on this shelf you find an unusual crystal like box. You can see right through it and it is empty. It has a sturdy lock. You pick it up. It is very strong. You lift the lid.

Now one by one, you put all of your cares in it... all the troubles and stress of your world.... Now put the lid back on. Lock it.... You put the box on the shelf. Somehow you know the box will stay there unnoticed in your private cove. If you ever need to look at its contents, you know you can come back to the cove and take out one by one, whatever you put in—just what you feel you can handle and no more... or you can leave it there forever.

You turn and find a nice spot. You sit down. You let the sand sift through your fingers. You feel so good... so peaceful... so relaxed — breathing — renewing... so relaxed.

Now you lie back. You feel the warmth along your spine, gradually, spreading comfortably over you like a blanket.

If you are using this tape as a sleep tape — you now drift off into a deep, refreshing sleep.... If not, leave the cove, climb over the rocks onto the beach. Once again the surf is pounding as you walk over to the spot where you left your shoes. Pick them up, clap them together, and brush the sand off yourself. You put on your shoes... and start to ascend the stairs. With each step upward, you find yourself more and more refreshed and energized. One — two — deeply breathe the warm moist ocean air — three — you are awakening — four — you feel so relaxed and so wonderful — five — wide awake — refreshed — really relaxed — energized!

Madeleine Cooper, L.C.S.W., is the clinical director of Mojave Mental Health in Las Vegas, Nevada. She received her M.S.W. from Fordham University School of Social Work.

18

Healing Breath

Guide: Karen M. Thomson

"Using the breath promotes relaxation and healing."

Introduction

Find a comfortable place to practice your meditation, perhaps outside (weather and privacy permitting) and maybe a couple of places inside. You may lie down or sit, as you prefer, so long as your spine, neck, and head are in a straight line and your whole body is relaxed. Lighting a candle, ringing a bell, burning some incense, or playing some soothing music can be used to signal that your meditation time has begun. Holding a rose quartz or an amethyst, or having a cross or a six-pointed star or any symbol or stone meaningful to you nearby can also be an aid in meditation. This is a favorite meditation in my Yoga and Meditation classes because of the wonderful relaxation and sense of well-being that it engenders.

The Journey

When you are ready to begin, assume your comfortable position with any of the aids to meditation you care to use (or none, if that is your preference). Close your eyes and begin to breathe very slowly and very deeply. As you keep your thoughts on your breathing, tune out all sensory perceptions. As other thoughts enter your mind to vie for your attention, gently acknowledge them and allow them to pass out of your mind as you silently witness any emotional or mental reaction. Your spiritual self, your higher self, your "God self" is completely in control now and your worldly self and thoughts have a "time out" during your meditations. Your meditation time is the all-important appointment you have made with yourself for your spiritual centering and rejuvenation. Thus, when other thoughts come to mind, acknowledge and release them consistently and with intent. Your quiet time now is top priority and when you return from your meditation, you will handle any responsibilities you have, probably better, having had the time to be refreshed and centered physically, emotionally, mentally, and spiritually through the meditation.

Breathe slowly and deeply for the next several minutes. With every breath that you take, feel yourself becoming more and more relaxed. As you inhale, imagine filling the body with Light, and energy, and all that is positive. As you exhale, let go of everything, and know that you are releasing toxins from the body, all anxiety and frustrations, and any darkness, disease, or discomfort.

Inhalations and exhalations are equally important, so breathe in deeply all that is positive, and exhale just as deeply the negativity that you do not want or need. Turning your thoughts within, focus all concentration on your breath. As you breathe in, breathe in God's Light and Love and healing power; as you breathe out, release, relax, and let go, totally and completely.

Imagine a ball of white Light above your head. This is a

sphere of swirling white Light, a healing Light. Imagine the top of your head opening as if it were a flower blossoming, like a lotus flower. On your next inhalation, breathe in the white Light through the top of your head, and as the Light flows into your head and down through your neck and shoulders, it brings with it a warm feeling. As the warm white Light gradually fills your body, it moves down the arms and out the finger tips. Exhale when you need to. As you continue to inhale, continue to breathe in the Light, which continues its way down your body: the upper chest, down the back and spine, down the stomach and pelvic area, the hips, the thighs. The Light that you are bringing into your body is healing, balancing, rejuvenating every cell in your body — every organ, bone, muscle, tendon, tissue, joint, all the body fluids — every part of your body. If there is any part of your body where there is discomfort, focus the Light there until you can see that part of the body filled and surrounded in Light, and completely well, healed and in harmony with the rest of the body. Continue breathing in the Light and seeing it moving down both legs, knees, calves, ankles, feet, and out the toes. See the body now as entirely filled with Light, and exhale, but continue to see the body full of Light, and peace, and love.

Again, breathe in deeply more of the Light so that the Light now not only fills the entire body, but also extends outward from the body a distance of several feet. See the body as filled and surrounded with this white, healing Light, which is protection, peace, love, and healing energy.

Notice how you feel now. Take a deep breath and feel how relaxed you are. Again, inhale, and give the body a good stretch as you tense every muscle in your body. Exhale and relax. Inhale and, again, stretch, tense every muscle as tightly as you can, and exhale and relax, let go. Be aware of your peaceful state and the deep sense of well-being that is a part of you. As you express gratitude for the benefits of the meditation you have just experienced, open your eyes. As you re-enter the world of human activity, feel a sense of renewal, a heightened consciousness, a wonderful sense of well being, which you can return to at any time simply by closing your eyes, taking a few very slow, deep breaths, and remembering the way you feel at this moment.

Karen M. Thomson, Ph.D., works in the University system of Georgia both as an administrator and a Professor of English. Concurrent with her academic career is her work as a New Age teacher/healer whose experiences during the past nearly twenty years have included lectures, classes, and workshops on Yoga and Meditation, Dream Interpretation, and Metaphysics, many through college adult Continuing Education Programs.

19

Meadow With Colors

Guide: Kay Henrion

"This meditation is for having fun and relaxing!"

Introduction

This meditation can be done using a variety of color. I have used blue for love, you may substitute pink for peace, green for healing, yellow for knowingness and learning, orange for wisdom, or violet for guidance. This is a wonderful imagery to use anytime you need to "escape" from tension. It's as if you are on a mini-vacation in your mind, and afterward you feel refreshed and ready to face your challenges.

The Journey

You are in a beautiful meadow. There is a clear blue sky above you. The grass is green and smells fresh and sweet. The trees around you are emerald green. There is a small flowing stream in the distance. You can hear it running over the rocks. You walk over to the stream and put your hand in the water. It is cool to touch and the wetness feels like silk on your hand. A soft breeze is blowing and you are filled with the feeling of love and peace. You lay on your back on the soft grass and let that feeling of love swirl around you like a soft whirlwind. It slowly lifts you up off the ground and towards the endless blue sky. The blue of the sky becomes deeper and deeper as you float higher and higher.

Pause

You are now in a space that is swirling in ever changing hues of blue from the deepest royal to the highest ice crystal blue. The swirling vibration of the blue colors support your body and enfold you in the wonderful feeling of love. As you allow your body to be immersed in this feeling, allow your mind to go into the silence and experience what is there for you.

Pause

It is time to come back. You are whole and complete. When you are ready open your eyes feeling refreshed and wide awake.

Kay Henrion is a Registered Nurse and a Family Nurse Practitioner in Naples, Florida. She specializes in holistic health counseling, offers seminars, and often lectures.

20

Relax

Guide: Pauline Fisher, B.S.M.A.

"A good imagery for body-part awareness."

Introduction

By integrating, varying, and personalizing many of my experiences, I found others interested in using the techniques I have developed through relaxation, meditation, and imagery. This visualization can be an outside guide for each person's own inner voice, and it helps in faster access to relaxation and sometimes sleep.

The Journey

Begin by removing or loosening anything binding such as jewelry and belts. Find a comfortable place and lie down on your back. Let your arms fall loosely by your side and uncross your legs and place them approximately in line with your hips. Take two or three slow deep breaths. As you do so, feel the breath in your body. Follow the breath in and out of your body. Follow the breath as it travels through the soles of your feet, through your calves and thighs and pelvis, your torso, and arms and neck... all the way up to your head and out again. Take another slow, deep breath all the way up to your head, and as your exhale, feel it exiting through the outer extremities of your fingers and your toes. Roll your head gently from side to side, releasing any tension. Do this a few times and then bring it back to center. Focus your attention on your body, your breath and the guide's voice.

Now, breathing normally, bring attention to your scalp. As you inhale, feel each of your hair follicles on your scalp. As you exhale, let go, relax, melt. Bring your awareness to your ears as you inhale. As you exhale, let go. Continuing to pay attention to your breath. Bring your awareness to your forehead, and as you exhale let go, relax, melt. And now your eyebrows as you inhale and as you exhale let go. Bring your attention to your eyelids, as you inhale, and as you exhale, relax, let go. If you have any difficulty keeping your eyes still while they are closed, try to focus on the bridge of your nose and that will help keep them still. Now bring your attention to your nose. Follow the path of your breath, in and out and let go of your nose. Bring your attention to your cheeks and your cheek bones, and as you exhale, relax, let go, melt like a surreal Salvador Dali painting, and now bring your attention to your jaw and if you find that you clench your teeth allow your mouth to open slightly and as you exhale let go, relax.

Bring your awareness to your lips and your mouth, your teeth, your gums and your tongue. As you exhale, let go, relax. Let your attention go to your widow's peak above the bridge of your nose at the hairline and imagine two lines from that point traveling around your hairline behind your ears to the nape of your neck, and around to your chin and into your mouth and follow that line as it travels along your gums, outside and inside, lower and upper. Bring your awareness now to your neck, outside and inside. The skin on the outside and everything else that is on the inside, and as you exhale, let go, feel your neck melting into the ground. Bring your attention to your shoulders. As you exhale, softly let go of the shoulders. Do it in your mind's eye. Let your mind just let go. Bring your awareness to your upper arms and elbows, outside and inside and as you exhale, relax, let go, melt. Bring your attention to your lower arms and wrists and let go of them. Now bring your awareness to your hands; the palms; the tops of your hands; and each and every finger starting with the right hand, the little finger, the ring finger, the middle finger, the index or pointing finger, and your thumb. Left hand, your thumb, your index finger, your middle finger, your ring finger, and your little finger. Bring your attention to your spine, starting at the very top and going vertebra by vertebra down the spine all the way to the coccyx. Let your mind run down your spine like fingers running across the keys of the piano... plink... plink... all the way down. Bring your awareness to your chest, your sternum and your rib cage, front and back. As you exhale, feel yourself melting into the floor. Bring your attention to your waist and your diaphragm and as you exhale allow that to melt into the floor, relax, let go.

In your mind's eye, see and feel your pelvis as if it were a vessel, imagine the top and the back part where most of the muscles of the body attach. As you softly exhale, let go, relax. Let go of the buttocks and the genitals and the joints where your legs attach to the torso. Feel the weight of your body, of the parts you have let go of. Become aware. Bring your attention to your thighs, inside and out and all around where the largest bone of the body is and let go. Relax your knees back and front. Feel the patella like the yoke of an egg and let it go letting your mind travel down to the lower legs, the calves, the shin bones and the ankles, relax each as you continue to the heels and the arches and the metatarsals, and the balls of the feet and each and every toe starting with the left foot: your little toe and the one next to it and the middle toe and the one next to it and your big toe... and your right foot: the big toe and the one next to it, and the middle toe and the one next to it and the little toe.

Now scan your body up and down. Let your mind's eye run up and down your body. If there are any places where you feel tension, breathe into it. Imagine your breath like bubbles of air breathing into the spot of tension and as you exhale, feel the tension flowing away. You might want to imagine white light into the spot or a Christmas tree ball. As you inhale and as you exhale see it breaking into a million pieces and floating out of your body. Feel the weight of your body on the floor. Become aware of where it is touching the floor... and where it is not touching. Is the floor holding you up or are you pressing into the floor? Just take note. No judgment, just be aware.

Pause

Imagine yourself on the beach. Feel the warmth of the sun and hear the sounds, possibly seagulls, the ocean, and waves. Smell the salt air; taste the salt air. Feel the impression your body makes in the sand. See the edge of the sea where little waves trickle on the beach; see the sun glistening like gems on the little waves. Allow the wave at the edge of the beach to touch your toes and slowly and gently let your body be carried out to a very calm sea. Slowly, slowly, feeling the coolness of the water under you and the warmth of sun above you. Be aware of the occasional splashes of water on the front of your body and feel the undulation of water under you. Allow your body to undulate in response. Be aware of how different your body feels floating on the water versus how it felt lying in the sand weighted. Continue to float. And now allow your mind to travel up to the sky and pick out one puffy white cloud, your cloud, and slowly let your body float up next to it. Floating, floating up and up. Travel with your companion cloud gently in the breeze and feel the difference of the floating in the air with a cloud versus floating in the water.

Pause

At the count of three, imagine your favorite place of relaxation, one you have been to before or one you can make up now in your mind's eye. Be sure when you get there that you see, feel, smell, hear, and taste all that is there. If it is indoors, be aware of where the electrical sockets are, the furniture, paintings on the walls. If it is outdoors, be aware of the colors and the weather. Be aware of your clothes and the textures under your feet. One... two... three... you are there. Take time to be totally there with all your senses. Remember: see, feel, smell, hear and taste all that is there. In this place, think of a word... your word... a word like *calm*, *peace*, or *love*. Feel that word within you, through all of your pores, throughout your bones and nerves and muscles and blood in each, and every part of you. Breathe it in, and when you breathe it out, share it. You are that word. Your aura becomes this word so that anyone who comes near you becomes this word with you.

Pause

Know that you can call upon this feeling whenever you like. Just close your eyes, take a few deep breaths and count down from three to one. Remember this feeling and know that you may come back to this place and time. It is yours.

When you are ready, gently bring your consciousness back to this place. Again, feel the floor beneath your body. Begin to hear peripheral sounds and let them drift in gently, gently. Let your arms slide on the floor over your head. Stretch as if you were on a stretching machine with your fingers going in one direction and your toes in the other and wiggle everything in between from your toes to your head, becoming aware of and awakening your whole body, front, back and sides. And when you are ready to sit or stand, roll over on your side bringing your knees to your chest and with as little tension as possible, continuing to be conscious of your breath and your body as well as your relaxed state of being.

Pauline Fisher, M.A., is a therapeutic movement educator and stress management consultant, as well as the author of a book. Her articles have been published here and abroad. She has been a recipient of many grants and is on the faculty of The University of Maryland. As the founder of A Moving Experience she does presentations and trainings throughout the United States and Canada. Her audiotape "Relaxation and Imagery" is available by writing to A Moving Experience, 1884 Columbia Rd. NW #105, Washington, D.C. 20009.

Accessing the Higher Self

21

Towers of Light

Guide: Ernestine Wolfe-Cline

"This meditation can bring one into a highly attuned state of awareness."

Introduction

As you move through the color spectrum of this imagery, you may feel its powerful imaging process intensify your higher perceptive abilities. You can become more sensitive as you continue to practice this exercise.

The Journey

Sit comfortably with your back straight, feet flat on the floor, and your hands in your lap with palms turned up. Breathe slowly and deeply allowing all the body muscles to relax. Allow the tensions of the day to drain away, leaving you feeling relaxed and at peace with yourself.

Mentally surround yourself in a large bubble of light. Bring your attention into the center of your being. Feel yourself in a quiet place. Sit quietly for a few moments. Become aware of the space around you, which is the universe. Find yourself surrounded by a beautiful midnight sky filled with stars and planets. Find yourself gently moving through this magnificent space.

Ahead of you is a light that draws you toward itself. As you approach it you begin to see the many colors which create the light.

You move closer and discover that each color is a great tower of light. You move upon the first tower which is red. Move upward to the top of the red tower. Dance upon it. Breathe the red into every cell of your being. Feel it.

Pause

Move now to the second tower of light. You find the orange light of this tower to be clear and radiant. Move through it—breathe it in. Taste it. Feel it. Allow the orange to flow through your being.

Pause

Now you find yourself drifting to the next tower of light, which is a clear jewel-toned yellow. Move to the top of the tower of yellow radiance. Drink it into your body. Feel it nourish every cell of your being.

Pause

It is time to move ahead to the next tower of light. You become aware of the beauty of the green light of this tower. The green is shining and gleaming with the jewel tones of emeralds. Allow its healing glow to move through all of the tissues of your body. Feel it. Absorb it into every cell.

Pause

Go forward now, to the next tower of light, which is a lovely blue like the noonday sky. Swim into the blue and move upward to the top of the tower of blue light. Feel it move through your being. Smell its fragrance. Experience the blue.

Pause

You find yourself drifting upward to the next tower of light which is indigo. The indigo is clear and jewel-toned. It is the color of a clear midnight sky. Dance through the indigo. Feel it. Breathe it into your being. Touch it. Smell it. Taste it.

Pause

Move forward to the next tower of light, which is violet. Clear, radiant and jewel tones as amethyst. Move into it and through it. Feel its pure texture. Draw it into your being. Feel its radiance and its healing energy.

Pause

As you stand upon the tower of violet, pure white light from above begins to spin around you. Allow it to spin as rapidly as you can. Finally you are totally surrounded by a spiral of pure white light. In this highly attuned state of awareness you remain in silence for awhile and move into your own experience.

Pause

When you are ready, gently allow the spiral of pure white light to carry you slowly and easily through each tower of colored light: violet, indigo — drifting slowly — blue, green, yellow, orange, and finally the clear jewel-toned red.

Find yourself in your quiet place. Begin to focus your attention on your breath. Breathe gently and easily. Allow your breath to assist you in bringing your awareness to your body. Move gently and comfortably as you return your awareness to your body and surroundings. Only when you are fully aware of your body and surroundings and feel comfortably ready, move back into your regular activities.

Ernestine Wolfe-Cline, who resides in Fort Myers, Florida, is a minister, artist, teacher and has used her intuitive and artistic abilities to assist others in their search for greater awareness and spiritual direction in their lives. She has developed a meditative process for creating artworks and teaching others to express their own creativity through drawing and painting. Her artworks are found in most of the fifty United States and eleven foreign countries.

22

Personal Solution

Guide: Lynn B. Robinson, Ph.D.

"Using this meditation allows you to tap into your total potential for clarity in problem resolution."

Introduction

The goal of this visualization is to become aware of alternative personal solutions to problems or challenges in your life. It was created to assist management and leadership clients in understanding and using their own creative problem solving powers. Results have been the creation of new ideas, synergistic solutions, and satisfaction with solutions in place. Use this imagery when the solution to a problem seems unclear or problematical.

The Journey

As you sit comfortably, relaxed in your chair, breathe slowly and deeply. Breathe in, allowing golden light to flow inward, and breathe out, expelling grey worn breath and thoughts. In with fresh, golden light; out with stale, darkened carbons. In with fresh insights, out with old ideas.

Continue breathing slowly, moving your consciousness away from your breath and to the whole of your body. Allow your consciousness to touch all parts of your body with the fresh invigorating breath you have taken in. Feel each cell of your body tingle with the newness of the moment. Know that you are alive and alert with the information you need, with the solutions you want.

With the knowledge of your knowing kept fully but tangentially in your consciousness, allow yourself to bring into focus a situation you want to resolve or a problem you'd like to solve. Feel it. See its dimension. Hear its parameters. Smell how it might smell. Taste it. Touch the problem in the form you have given it. Now allow the form to change, accepting a new form to the problem, sensing it in new ways. Let it change form again. If the form is scary, imagine it as loving. How does it look, taste, feel, smell, sound?

As you get to know this problem or situation in its many possible forms, embrace it with appreciation. Wrap it in waves of thanks for the opportunity it gives you to grow and to know more and more and more.

Now that you know the problem well, sense it changing to resolution, to solution. See, hear, touch, feel, smell that solution. Allow yourself a few moments to get to know the newness of the old problem in its shape and form of solution.

Keeping the solution in your awareness, experience yourself moving from the form of the old problem to that of its solution. Be conscious of the things you are doing, the things you are saying that move you on the journey from problem to solution. Get in touch with the environment that allows the change. Use all of your senses to become familiar with your path from problem to solution. Experience that environment externally with the people and things around you.

Experience that environment internally with the thoughts and emotions within you.

Now return very briefly to the old problem. Recognize it and begin to re-experience your journey to solution, allowing your consciousness to linger where it feels the need. Move on toward your solution and take a few minutes to re-experience it in the fullness of its satisfaction. Gather a few more impressions if you need them.

Begin now to quicken your breathing and become aware again of your physical body. Shift your awareness to physical environment around you. Consciously enjoy the rewards of your problem solution imagery. Job well done!

Lynn Robinson is a management consultant in Mobile, Alabama and Professor Emeritus of Marketing at Southern University. She has an impressive list of degrees in business administration and works as an "intuitive" facilitator.

23

Winter Seeds

Guide: Annette Covatta

"The power of meditation is in discovering and exploring the seeds of life found in darkness."

Introduction

By using the symbology of winter, this imagery has, for me, unlocked doors to latent energies of being and has connected me to my heart as "home." At meditation workshops, some people are deeply stirred by this visualization and work with it for extended periods of time.

The Journey

Let your eyes close. Be aware of the darkness. Sink into it. There is nothing to fear. When your heart is open, the darkness becomes peaceful and inviting. Try to feel the tone and quality of this darkness. What sensations does it evoke?... heaviness?... thickness?... softness?... lightness?... Feel the sensations as they float in and out of your body. Once more, sink into the darkness. It is not static. It slowly transforms itself into a silence.. a stillness of your inner self. When you feel connected to this inner quiet... this silent moment... bring your attention to your breathing... the rhythmic movement of breathing in and out... inhale... exhale... one whole breath... being at one with the breath....

Now go inside your heart, wherever you imagine your heart to be. Enter your heart-center, that place of being "home" where your deepest longings and dreams reside as well as your true feelings and dark secrets. All of life, with its changing seasons, passes through your heart, our place of true, inner knowing.... Your heartland is your homeland. We find in our deepest center springtime's birthing.... summertime's flowering... autumntime's maturing harvest and wintertime's gestating darkness. The four cycles/seasons can co-exist all at the same time in the heart.

You are inside your heartspace now. The whole universe is before you there. The winds, rains, oceans, fires and earth... sun and moon... vibrant colors, vegetation, flowers, autumn leaves, and white snow.

Spend some time in that space of your heart that represents winter. Follow the pathway that brings you to the winter stillness, whiteness, and frozenness. Feel the cold on your skin even as you take in the glistening magic with your eyes. The soil is hard. But, as you become one with the winter elements, the soil begins to soften. As you gradually sink down, down,... deeper and deeper, into the ground, below the surface, into the darkness of the soil.

You are not afraid. There is a mystery and wonderment in the dark, quiet depths of the wintery soil. The darkness is not negative or disturbing. It is creative and beckoning.

As you settle into the warmth of the underground terrain, you notice a number of seeds nestled in the soil. Each seed is alone in its own circled space. No two are the same. They are motionless, seemingly lifeless. But, you know that they are in the womb-like process of becoming. Each seed, is in a different stage of its life, lying dormant below the frozen earth… each seed holding potential of life. One is, so fragile. Will it survive the winter? Another is so hardy that its yellow blossom pierces through the darkness, smiling on the white snow-blanket above. There are seeds of all shapes and sizes simply taking a long winter's rest. But, you know that their rest is a quiet state of pregnancy.

Focus on these winter seeds that are in your heart. Choose one to explore… to attend to. Find a comfortable place in the winter spot of your heart where you can sit down. Bring your attention to your life at this moment… situations, dilemmas… blockages… relationships, job/work, your body, life's meaning…. What circumstance of your life feels like this seed? Put a name on it. Perhaps the seed of physical pain… loneliness… fear of abandonment… companioning a dying loved one… grieving a loss… a seed of insecurity… some fear… overwork… misunderstanding….

As you name the seed, pick it up. Let your senses of sight, smell, touch, hearing, and taste relate to it. Tell it that you accept it in your present life. This may be hard to do. Accepting our reality is the first step toward changing the reality. It clears the channel for the seed to be transformed and to grow. Now tell the seed how you feel about its presence in your life. Simply honor your feelings by naming them. Take all the time you need to explore the winter seed that is calling your attention.

Pause

Now, return the seed back into the soil of your heart. Sit

quietly for a few moments, feeling fully your feelings. Make a promise to nurture the soil of your heart in its wintertime season.

Pause

You are now being drawn upward through the dark terrain into the light of your heart center. Pause a bit on the threshold of your heart and drink in the beauty and wonders of all that your heart holds....

When you feel ready to come back to the room, open your eyes slowly and feel yourself refreshed and energized.

Annette Covatta, D.M.A., has a lifetime involvement in the arts and personal growth programs, and she holds a Doctor of Musical Arts from Boston University. Ms. Covatta is the founder and director of FULCRUM, an organization whose mission is to enable persons to reach their potential through the body/mind/spirit/soul connection. Through FULCRUM, she presents workshops which reflect her interest in the creative process and wholistic spirituality.

24

Wisdom Dream

Guide: Karen Carnabucci

"Discover a new awareness of your relationship with your higher power."

Introduction

This journey was created for individuals who wish to expand their senses of their higher powers and their experiences of accessing the wisdom of such powers. It is designed in a non-threatening setting, and listeners usually report positive feelings of clarity or reassurance. I have often used this imagery at the closure of workshops or gatherings of groups. It is also very useful as a warm-up exercise prior to longer meditations that might include extended contact with the wisdom figure for writing in a journal.

The Journey

Close your eyes, breathe in deeply to relax and allow your breathing to become even and regular....

Become aware, as you continue to breathe, of a soft blanket of sparkling white light and golden and silver threads that is now at your toes. Begin now to slowly and gently pull this magical blanket over your feet, your legs, your pelvic area and midsection, and now your chest, until this blanket rests softly at the tip of your chin....

Pause

You are now aware of feeling extremely relaxed yet alert. Feel yourself now slowly awakening in the middle of the night in your own bedroom at home. As you look around the bedroom, your eyes adjusting to the light of the lamp beside your bed, you notice familiar objects. Then you see something different, unfamiliar, something that you can't believe you've ever noticed before — a small door at one end of the room that invites your curiosity....

You decide to rise and investigate this door, taking the bedside lamp with you. You are aware now of your bare feet on the floor as you move to that door. Notice that as your lamp light floods over this space, you can see more distinctly, the quality of that door, its weight and shape, its decoration or lack of decoration, and the doorknob, which appears to contain in its center a precious jewel.

Pause

Turn the doorknob of this door and bend your head as you open it and step to the other side. Find yourself stepping into blackness, your lamp lighting only the first step of a stairway in front of you.... You decide to take the stairway, climbing each step one by one. Notice how it feels to move up the stairs and if you have any thoughts or feelings about what your are doing or where you are going.... You find yourself at a landing now, and take a moment to rest. Notice the quality of the floor and how it feels against your feet....

Then you realize that another stairway is ahead of you, and again you take each step. This stair feels less narrow than the first; notice your feelings as you continue to climb, the next step, and the next step, and the next.

Pause

Now you find yourself at a second landing, noticing the feelings that are present now as you pause... the lamp casts its glow on the first step another stair ahead of you, and after a moment, you continue upward, step by step. The stairs seem even wider now, and it seems as if you can't touch the walls with your hands. Notice the feelings as you continue to climb....

At the final step, you find yourself at a third landing and see there is a large door in front of you. It is still dark, but you can see a sliver of light shining from the place where the door edge and the floor meet. The light of your lamp shines on the doorknob of this door, and you judge it to be a beautiful and precious jewel. As you stand at this door, notice how it feels to be here....

You decide to enter this room, turning the knob and walking through the doorway. Ahead you see a chair, and on that chair, a figure whose wisdom and guidance you are seeking.... The figure gestures that you draw closer, and you now see an identical chair sitting in front of this figure that you know is meant for you.... You take the seat and allow yourself to feel the presence of this wisdom figure.... Form now the question you wish to have answered.... Wait for the reply that comes.... If the answer appears unclear, ask for more information.

Pause

You become aware that the figure has a gift for you, and you extend your hand to take it, then carefully place it in your pocket.... After processing your gratitude, you pick up the lamp that you have brought with you. You realize that it is time to leave this place, and you know that you can visit at any time you wish, since now you know the way. Turning now, you close the door behind you and begin your descent, taking each step carefully, aware of the special gift in your pocket.

Now you find yourself at the small doorway that you first entered, and open that door, remembering to bend your head as you pass through. Your bedroom is quiet and dark, with everything as you left it. You return to the side of your bed, placing the lamp at the bedside. You touch your pocket and discover the gift is still there. You now swing your legs back into the bed and pull the covers over you as you fall into a deep and comfortable sleep....

Become aware of the morning sunlight at the window and begin to move and stretch your body now, as you prepare to awaken. When you feel ready, open your eyes and return to this room.

Karen Carnabucci is a therapist specializing in experiential therapies, including psychodrama, family sculpture, and imagery, in her work with adult children of alcoholics and dysfunctional families. A former newspaper writer and editor, she is a consulting therapist at Caron Family Services, affiliated with the Caron Foundation, an internationally recognized drug and alcohol treatment center in Wernersville, Pa. She recently collaborated on a book, "Intimacy, The Quest for Connection."

Peace

25

Into The Forest

Guide: Nancy Harn-Wagner

"This visualization is to assist you in finding the inner peace available when connecting with the earth by visiting the woods."

Introduction

After a day in the city, surrounded by cement and traffic, this visualization is especially helpful in connecting with the earth. If possible play some recordings of woodland sounds as you practice this journey.

The Journey

Come to the edge of the forest, close your eyes... ask permission to enter and begin your transformation.

Take a moment to breathe in the aroma of the earth's richness beneath your feet. Slowly, take in long deep breaths of the refreshing tranquility you have longed for. Take a few minutes to fill your lungs with the vitality of moist pine and cedar scents and visualize the beauty all around you. As you begin to relax, acknowledge the inner peace you experience as you nourish your body with fresh, clean air.

Pause

Visualize a beautiful white light in your heart center — see it expanding throughout your entire body and feel this white light of protection projecting to the area around you.

Now look around you. Enjoy the canopy of protection above you formed by towering trees — shielding you and offering strength as you begin to settle into this temple of beauty built by nature for all of its creatures to enjoy. Feel the security of being alone yet know that there is a warmth of love all about you. Observe the scurrying of birds in dry leaves searching for food, the rustle of small animals and insects accepting your presence. Because you come in peace, they feel no threat by your existence. Be thankful for this moment in time and enjoy the happiness of birds fluttering above as though angels of protection were over you.

Observe the growth in plants and vines and shrubs; see that growing process as it happens. Know that your inner growth develops as surely and steadily — each depending on nourishment from the earth's energy. Notice the strength that seeps into your veins as you marvel at the power in this forest and you begin to sense that this is where you belong.

As you look about, take time to absorb the spirit of the forest and begin to listen. Hear the sounds of nature's woodland, and let your body acknowledge the rhythm of movement that surrounds you; allow it to become a part of your heartbeat.

Feel the drums beat as blood pumps through your body, and the energy that rushes through you gives force to your very being. Know that the trembling which you feel is your connection to the spirit. Lift your face to the dew drops falling from lush greenness and accept this healing. Feel peace in the birds' songs and happiness in your heart as their music resounds magically through the woods.

With your hand touch the dampness of the leaves, the textures of the rough barks, the softness of the birds' wings as you are allowed to clutch these blessings of nature to your heart. Rest for a moment on the cool rock before you and take in its energy as you observe the happiness of clean water winding its way in the creek near your feet. Sit here a moment and absorb the beauty of this place and this time in your life.

As you return to the edge of the forest where you began your journey, know that this memory is one you may return to anytime you wish. Recalling the thought of this environment will help you during any time of difficulty. Open your eyes when you are ready and go in peace.

Nancy Harn-Wagner is a professional visionary artist and writer who resides in Clearwater, Florida.

26

Peace of Mind

Guide: Mona O'Neal

"Creating a pocket of internal peace by changing the level of consciousness can prove physically therapeutic, mentally inspirational, and spiritually healing."

Introduction

This journey into higher consciousness puts our concerns into perspective and provides the peace through which to access divine guidance. It can calm inner turmoil whenever there is external agitation, frustration, or troubling questions to which answers appear non-existent. It is also helpful before sleep. The blue water image can relieve the sense of urgency about an external situation and create a feeling of peace. The ascension gradually allows gigantic problems to diminish. It is also available in a tape series "Meditation in the Real World," which provides opportunity for greater relaxation with a soothing musical background.

The Journey

Effective imagery depends largely on a relaxed body and mind. Settle into a comfortable position and loosen any restrictive clothing. Begin deep, relaxing breaths with eyes gently closed. Tense the muscles of your toes and feet... and relax. Now tense the calf and thigh muscles... and relax.

Move up to the lower torso, tense every muscle hold it... and relax. Take a deep breath, hold it... and relax. Tighten muscles in the chest, hold then relax, so relaxed.... Tense your arm and hand muscles, hold and let go. Take another deep breath... hold... and let it go. Now tighten the muscles in your face and in your jaws... and let it go... let it all go.... Breathe deeply once more and mentally tighten the muscles in your mind where you have held all those stressful thoughts... hold on tight... and now let them go.

It is safe here... nothing can intrude, nothing can disrupt. See your mind as a deep, blue lake of clear, unruffled water... reflecting all the universe in its surface like a mirror.... Let it remain perfectly still for just a moment... Feel your whole being immersed in this depth of peaceful, relaxed stillness.... Absorb its calm, healing essence into every muscle, every cell and atom of your body, into every recess of your mind.... This peace is now washing away all confusion... all concern... cleansing all negative emotion... transforming all fear into faith... allow this relaxing purification to engulf you as you feel each care... completely dissolved into this heavenly, healing peace.

Pause

When you feel yourself totally renewed, in perfect peace, step from the brilliant, blue water onto the shore, where you find a golden robe. Wrap yourself lovingly and gently in its richness and walk toward a waiting rainbow-colored hot air balloon. This is a space balloon, and your golden robe is your space suit. The balloon and your space-robe provide you with complete comfort and absolute safety. Feel the exhilaration and the honor as you step aboard.... As the balloon begins its ascent up over the trees, watch the striking beauty and peace of the countryside. From here the farmer in his field looks like a charming, rustic painting. Greet the curious birds who have left their nests behind to enjoy a race with your rainbow balloon.

Pause

Climbing higher now, the farmer's field and all the other fields join together, to create a beautiful patchwork quilt of rich browns and greens and yellows, trimmed with bright and glistening blue rivers and lakes, and soft, white clouds in the distance. From here all the little field mice problems, the tractor repairs, the broken fences, are simply melted into one glorious scene. From this level, all is serenity and beauty, harmony and peace. Rising higher now, you are passing right through the center of a brilliant rainbow. Its cool mist caresses your skin... your balloon colors merging with its colors, your energy merging with this gentle miracle of nature... and you are inspired, and lifted, higher still.

Pause

And now you have an astronaut's view of the earth. Our glorious sphere of radiant blue water and lands with no borders traveling in perfect order in it's perfect path...

Pause

...and you rise upward still, until you move among the stars... timeless... birthless... deathless... and all is open, all is free. You are boundless, yet wholly united with every vibration of the universe. Breathe deeply and rest in this expanded state for just a moment.

Pause

Before you return, decide how much of this peace, this freedom you will bring back into your outer life. How much of it are you willing to trade for the cares you left behind, invisible now from this height.

No problem can ever be solved from the level of the problem, but you are now in a higher level... with all the intelligence of the universe in your grasp. Ask for the solution, in a form that you can understand and know that it will come.

Pause

Now we must leave this time and place of perfect serenity. You may choose to bring this feeling of peace back into your outer world, or you can return here again and again until the two levels merge, and you become this perfect peace.

As the rainbow balloon makes its descent, thank your balloon captain for this grand adventure... drop the golden robe to the floor and see that you are wearing your regular clothes.... Take a deep breath and feel your body tingling with the joy of aliveness.... Wiggle your fingers and toes, and move your shoulders. Open your eyes and be here now, wide awake, alert and feeling wonderful, in perfect peace, right where you are.

Mona O'Neal is a Religious Science Practitioner, a writer, and the producer of workshops on meditation and self-esteem. She is the creator of a tape series, "Meditation in the Real World," of which these journeys are a part.

27

Peaceful Void

Guide: Larry Moen

"Fear not for the Void is your friend."

Introduction

It is so difficult for many of us to do nothing. Most of us are caught in the activity of life, and when we find ourselves with nothing to do, we try immediately to fill that moment instead of enjoying and treasuring it. This meditation will help you become comfortable with the Void, the Nothingness, the Peace and Quiet of your own being. This meditation should be done many times, because achieving that Peaceful Void is not easy if your life is full of distractions and motion. Try it and do not become frustrated. You have spent a lifetime accumulating distractions, and you cannot expect to leave them behind without a little patience and practice.

This meditation is best initially practiced in a place and at a time where you will encounter the least distractions. As you become more and more comfortable in the realm of Nothingness, you will find that you can release this Feeling within you whenever you choose.

The Journey

Close your eyes and take a deep breath. Inhale a green cloud... and exhale a leaf falling gently.... As you inhale, the rising green cloud floats higher and higher.... As you exhale the leaf floats down gently.... Inhale the rising green cloud... and exhale the gentle falling leaf....

If you cannot see the color, then visualize the word green. Look at each letter G-R-E-E-N. Now see the entire word green. The word green now becomes the color green. Now gently glide green into your heart center. Let your heart center accept it and radiate green from it. Allow green to soak into your compassionate heart and make the exchange of love with green. Both become one at this time.

Imagine a glowing green light in your heart center that will be with you during this meditation. Take a few moments now to feel and experience this calming, cooling and soothing green glow as it emanates from your heart center.

Pause

Now acknowledge unfulfilled desires of illusion and fantasy regarding outside people, objects or addictions. They are something your desire. Transform these desires into thoughts.

Sink the thoughts down into your chest. Move them out of your mind and into the lower part of your body. Make the thoughts reality in your being. Transform the thoughts into transparent particles and bursts of clear energy. Imagine your thoughts one by one transforming into nothingness, into the void.

Feel this void. Describe the void in detail. See its shape, size, color, thickness, weight, taste, and smell. Feel it again.

Pause

Now take the green light of love that has been soaking in your heart center and use it to caress the void. Treat it kindly and affectionately, as you would the outside person or object. Outside material and objects and inside emotions may try from time to time to enter this void. Recognize their importance and gently let them know that the void is a place for nothing, and that they may pass through and vanish. And know they will not disturb the void.

Draw the void closely to you. Hug it; stroke it lovingly and gently welcome it into your body.

Allow the void to float within you. It is your friend. It may feel awkward at first. That's O.K. Don't try to fill the space. Enjoy the emptiness and joy. Just let the void exist and become the love that embraces it.

When you feel you have experienced all that is necessary for now, bring yourself back to a conscious state.

Larry Moen is the editor and driving force behind the Meditations *series. As a Vietnam veteran, Mr. Moen has been aware that significant emotional events can influence one's life. Mr. Moen discovered that past programming from childhood forward can be healed and transformed using the powers of guided meditation. Subsequently, Mr. Moen embarked on an intensive study of guided visualization which he incorporates in his work with T'ai Chi, yoga and self-hypnosis. He currently leads meditation groups and speaks at seminars.*

28

Rain

Guide: Eleanor K. Sommer

"Find quiet time, and your world will change."

Introduction

Technology should be a tool in our lives like anything else. It should be part of a greater system that offers food for the soul as well as the table. Unrelenting growth has made us forget how healing and relaxing our natural world can be. The power of nature is awesome, and we should not seek so much to control as to respect, understand, and be a part of it. This meditation is for learning to recognize the relationship we have with our environment. It is to help you remember to stop what you are doing and to focus on something simple like a bird singing, an ant crawling across a ledge, or the rain gently falling outside your window.

Although this guided imagery can be practiced when you are removed from natural settings, remember to find moments in your life when you can relate simply and quietly to any part of your natural environment that brings you joy and contentedness. You don't need any special tools or chants to achieve that peace. It is inside of you. You just need to be quiet enough to access it.

The Journey

Still your mind and open an imaginary window. Listen to a breeze blowing gently through some wind chimes. Relax at your desk... at your kitchen table... or while standing in line at the bank. Wherever you are, it is now possible to take just a few minutes to relate to something other than progress, money, or consumption. Allow yourself the privilege of doing nothing. Your work, children, spouse, or other distractions can wait a few moments.

Open the window, and inhale the moist cool air that precedes a summer shower. Hear the birds twittering and cooing as the clouds gather on the horizon. Hear the breeze rustle the trees, and feel it brush across your face and skin. Inhale and exhale the cool, relaxing air. Open the window wider and lean out letting the smells of gathering clouds permeate your nostrils. Inhale and exhale...slowly, contentedly. You have nowhere to go... nothing to do but enjoy the coming storm.

The breeze begins to stir more strongly, rushing past your face and tickling your ears... perhaps billowing your clothing and messing up your hair. Enjoy the feeling of contact with wind, listen to it shake the trees, and watch as it turns the leaves upside down so that their silvery undersides dance and glitter in the fading sunlight.

Imagine now that a little bit of rain begins to fall. One drop. Then another. Here and there. Begin to notice the drops as they fall on the leaves and then to the ground. Feel the drops on your face and hold out your hands to try to catch the intermittent drops as they fall to the earth. Now you begin to smell a musty, earthy odor as the rain wets the earth, grass, trees and leaves. Perhaps your rain is falling on a sidewalk or rooftop, and you can feel the hot steam rise as the drops evaporate.

It is beginning to rain harder, and you decide to duck your head back inside where you can enjoy the breeze and the smells without getting completely soaked. Now focus all your senses on the rain. Hear it increasing in intensity and feel the spray as the wind blows it in the window. Hear it passing through the trees and falling on the ground or sidewalk.

You are excited as the sound is magnified and all you hear now is rain roaring in your ears. Pounding, thundering rain all around you. Inhale and exhale remaining calm and restful as the rain thunders around you. Relax and enjoy and respect the power of this natural event.

Pause

Notice now that the rain is beginning to subside. The sky is getting lighter, and a few birds have bravely ventured out and are singing in loud shrill voices. Listen as the rain falls in a gentler, softer way. The wind is gone and in its place a cool, fresh breeze blows in through the window and lingers around your body. Feel the coolness. Relax and inhale this clean, invigorating air. Notice now that the sun is beginning to shine from behind the clouds, and the rays begin to warm the drooping flowers and plants. As the sun awakens the flowers, they begin to release their fragrances, and the cool, refreshing air is now filled with the smells of flowers. Inhale and exhale the cool clean air. Feel refreshed and revitalized and ready to return to your work.

Be thankful that you can stop anytime or anywhere that you wish and take part in this scene in your imagination or as a part of your everyday reality. Remember to find some moments each day to relax and enjoy the natural environment around you — real or imagined.

Eleanor K. Sommer is a writer, free-lance editor, and publishing and communications consultant who lives in Naples, Florida.

Transformation & Growth

29

Anger Release Through Forgiveness

Guide: Mona O'Neal

"Once expressed, anger can be a healthy motivation for change."

Introduction

Much violence in today's society is due to inappropriate and long delayed expression of anger. Old anger is a deadly guest. This exercise expresses and expels him forever and begins the healing process by setting you free. It is important for this visualization that you can continue through to the end without being interrupted. This imagery provides a setting of safety within which you can vent old or immediate anger. This will help express, explode, and extinguish its destructive powers. Once you have vented your powerful anger on the object of your rage to the point of destruction, there is an immediate release, followed by a feeling of guilt. This is the perfect moment of forgiveness which should be expressed without acting out a "victim" role.

The Journey

Find a place and a position which is most comfortable for you. Your complete relaxation is very important for effective imagery. So sit or lie down, take several deep, cleansing breaths and force the air out of your lungs. Tighten the muscles of your feet and legs and hold it... now let go... limp and relaxed. Take a deep breath and blow it out. Now, tighten the muscles of your lower body, as tight as you can and hold it... let go... and breathe... relaxed... so relaxed. Now the upper body, your arms down to your fingertips, tighten every muscle as hard as you can and hold it... relax, breathe deeply... so relaxed. Tighten the muscles in your face and jaw, your neck and ears, even your scalp as tight as you can and hold it... and let go; let it all go completely.... Take a slow relaxing breath and let it go.... Your whole body now feels completely relaxed, completely at peace. Take a slow, deep breath, and as it leaves your body, let it carry all remaining tension with it. Relaxed.... So relaxed....

See yourself in a comfortable room. There is someone with you, someone with whom you feel absolutely safe, unconditionally loved. This is your guard and your guide, who is here to protect and support you as you confront the object of your anger. You are perfectly safe.

Now, put your image of the person who has made you so angry in front of you. See all his/her features in your mind. Feel his presence. Make it come alive and real. Your guard is here to protect you. There is nothing to fear. See the object of your anger clearly, watch his chest rise and fall with his breathing. As you look at this person, use your mind like a heat sensor and scan your own body, for any area of tension or discomfort. As you look at this person, with your mind, feel carefully along each inch of your body.

What you are finding is the place or places where you have stored the fire of your anger. This anger when kept locked away, is like the smoldering fires of hell. Even from outside the locked doors the acrid smell assaults your nostrils... on your skin, you sense the burning heat from the other side of the door. A bitter taste fills your mouth as you feel the heat rising within you... you are becoming your anger!

Now, with your guide just behind at your left shoulder, giving you complete permission and protection... tell this person you face, how you feel.... It's okay to be angry; you have every right to feel this anger. Tell him so... tell him what he did to you... and how much it hurt you or upset you... what he did to your life!

Pause

Tell him what you expected from him and how he let you down. Look him straight in the eyes and tell him all the things you have wanted to say ever since.... It's okay, this is the time to say it all... to feel it all. Tell him... your guard is here, nothing can harm you. Once the truth of your feelings is out, you can be free of this fiery cauldron of rage. Tell him everything... and as you tell it all, feel all the heat of your anger rising up from within, until you feel you are completely filled with all your anger

Now... Right now, allow this anger to blast through the locked doors of every cell in your body and shoot forth like a laser beam from your eyes, destroying... utterly vaporizing the image before you.... There is nothing left. Nothing....

Your guide gently comforts you and nods in approval. You rest for a moment in release. Your old anger has now been expressed and expelled in the purifying, white heat of the laser, and your body is left cleansed, released, and free. Relax and breathe easily and freely and feel the newness and peace surrounding you. Notice that even the room has now changed. It is light and airy and looks like a nursery.

What you have just destroyed is your image of that person for whom you had such anger. The essence of that person, which is pure and perfect spirit, is eternal.... Here in this spiritual nursery you find that inner essence lying in a crib, cooing and smiling and reaching up to you. This perfect child, a creation of God, needs your love and forgiveness.

Lift the infant spirit to your shoulder now. Hold it tenderly and let its incredible softness touch your cheek and fill your heart with pure compassion and forgiveness. You can see that this spirit is a growing thing on its own path, in its own struggle toward the light, just as you are. Here, you know that it is not necessary for you to forgive the behavior of this child, and you know that you need never subject yourself to that behavior ever again. With your inner wisdom, separate the essence of this pure spirit, which you now hold gently to you, from all that has gone before... and whisper, "All that is over now. I will put no more energy into my old image of you. I forgive you." As you place this precious spirit child once again in the crib, softly say to it... and within your innermost being...," All is forgiven, I release you now to your own good, as I am free to mine."

Turn away now to find your guide waiting. Walk hand in hand through the door, closing it securely behind you. As you walk out into the sunshine of a perfect... new... spring day. Thank your guide and say good-bye.... Breathe in the freedom of this place... deeply and allow its healing light to fill every cell. Breathe in the newness of this moment and know that you are free!

30

Climbing the Mountain

Guide: Janet Doucette

"As you climb the mountain you can leave behind what no longer works or is not needed."

Introduction

I use this journey in workshops to explore the subject of "Taking Responsibility." Where do we hold our fears? What are our bodies telling us? How can we learn to let go of old patterns and habits? This journey permits us to let go of that which binds us, and it allows us to experience our Higher Selves. This visualization can be repeated as often as anxiety or tension rules your life. It provides a balancing opportunity and helps you see priorities.

The Journey

Begin with mindful breathing. Sit straight with your spine erect and hands placed gently upon your thighs. As you breathe allow the breath to spiral down through your body, nourishing your cells and organs. Relax and release, into the exhaled breath, and out into the white light that surrounds you, the toxins and the tensions accumulated during the day. Sense your chakra energy centers opening one by one, spinning freely in a clockwise fashion.

You see that you are standing at the base of a great mountain. Its tall cliffs and rugged rock faces beckon you. The summit is shrouded in mist, and its base hidden by a thick forest. There is a path before you now, which leads into this forest. You are determined to climb to the top of this mountain.

You have come prepared for this journey. Upon your shoulders is a heavily laden backpack with food, utensils, clothing, and a tent. All of the things you require to live in the woods and all of the mountaineering equipment you will need to negotiate the cliffs, are packed tightly within the sack you carry on your back. Your expensive hiking boots are the best that can be purchased. You have spared no expense, no effort in preparing for this achievement.

Placing the backpack securely upon your back, you step confidently on the forest path. You have decided to ascend the White Cross trail and you carry a map, though the way is well marked. The path deepens into the forest and you detect the subtle incline of the trail.

After many miles, the pack is growing heavy but you have the inner strength to persevere. You hear the sounds of thundering waters. The trail is leading up now, past a mountain cascade several hundred feet high. You stop at a pool at the bottom of the falls and stare at the rushing water that swirls across the rocks. This runoff feeds many streams that lead to many rivers. There is a message for you in this pool. Look carefully into the icy, cold, raging waters.

Pause

You are now ready to ascend the first rock face on the White Cross Trail. It is the perpendicular face of the cliff over which the waterfall plunges. You begin the climb by steadying your pack. You place your hands on the fingerholds and begin the climb. It is difficult and steep. The pack feels heavier now that you are balanced by finger and toe holds. As you pull yourself to the ledge below the top of the cliff, you realize that you can physically go no further.

The weight of the pack is too great. There is not even enough room on the ledge to rest. There is only enough space to wedge your body uncomfortably in the cracks. You see that you must lighten your load in order to climb higher. Whatever you leave behind will remain upon the ledge until you return on the descent. It is a question of what you wish let go of, what you no longer truly need on this climb.

Pause

Open your backpack now and see that there is more in your backpack than you imagined. There are many more things than those required for camping and climbing. Reach in and remove the first object your hand touches.

Pause

What does it mean to leave this behind you?

Pause

Trusting that you can retrieve it later if desired, place the object upon the ledge and return the pack to your back. Lighter now, you find the ascent to the cliff top much easier. Continuing now upon the White Cross Trail, you follow the narrow mountain stream to a large rockslide. You must begin another difficult part of the climb.

You scramble up the massive boulders and still the climb is higher. There is a narrow rock ledge upon which you may walk, but the pitch is vertical and the height staggering to your senses. As you begin the steep ascent around the curve of the cliff, you realize that the path has narrowed considerably. In order to continue, you must swing out around the edge. You realize that the size of your pack is too great and will upset your balance. The force of gravity and the imbalance will cause you to fall over the precipice.

You can see the summit of the mountain from this rocky ledge. Wispy clouds encircle it and it is barren. It is a place of somber beauty. It is a place of origins and of wisdom. In order to continue the climb, you must traverse this ledge. You are again required to search the contents of your pack. What can you leave behind in order to continue? Is there something you feel you need, but no longer want?

Pause

As you decide what item you will no longer carry, you are filled with a greater sense of purpose. What possessed you to pack so many unnecessary things and how heavy the burden of carrying them has been. Decide now, what other things you wish to let go of. If there is a behavior, a way of thinking, a great loss that grieves you, or an anger that no longer serves a purpose, release them now.

Pause

You are ready now for the final ascent to the summit of this mountain you have chosen to climb. You are much lighter now, your body movements are more free, and unencumbered. You can place your hands in the fingerholds more easily. You traverse the ledge and begin the upward climb. You are above the treeline and can see for miles around you. But you are focused on the climb. It is you and the mountain face.

The cliff face to the summit is deceptive; the toe holds are too narrow to hold securely. You are within sight of the top but cannot reach it. The steel shanked toes of your boots are too thick, too clumsy, to get a tight grip. You are reaching down and untying the laces. Leaving them behind on the cliffs no longer concerns you. With bare feet and renewed strength, you pull yourself up the final feet of the unimaginably difficult climb.

Pause

Now, at long last, you are standing on the summit. As you look below, you see that the sun is low in the afternoon sky — soon it will be sunset, and you will watch the moon rise from the plains below.

Take a long breath, and see before you now — an eagle soaring. Within the eyes of that eagle, there is great wisdom. The way has been difficult, and you have had to sacrifice much. Take a few moments now too look at yourself clearly, through the eagle's eyes. Realize the things within that need to be transformed, and recognize the courage you now have to perform that difficult task.

Pause

You did not need to conquer the mountain in order to reach the summit, you only needed to become One with it. And you have never needed to conquer your fear and attachments, you have only needed to lay them aside in order to experience yourself, as you truly are, through the eyes of the Eagle.

Pause

Stay on the summit for as long as you wish. Feel the hard surface beneath you, a foundation of strength to sustain you.

Pause

When you are ready to leave the mountain, flex your newborn wings and leap. Soaring down to the valley below, you are now free.

Janet Ware Doucette uses guided imagery and cross-cultural healing techniques in workshops and support groups in order to enable others to experience their higher selves. A profound near-death experience in 1986 left her with an awareness of our abilities to heal ourselves.

31

Home

Guide: Liz Bachtel, MA

"In the Jungian archetypes, house symbolizes 'self.'"

Introduction

The process of self-realization can be enhanced and aided by imagery based on Carl Jung's archetypal symbols. In this imagery, I have used the symbol of the "house" as "self". This visualization creates a wonderful opportunity for discussion and analysis through the details presented by the client. Besides its deeper purpose of helping clients with personal growth and development, this visualization is also simply enjoyable and relaxing — an effective and instant mini-vacation.

The Journey

Position yourself comfortably in a chair with your feet flat on the floor, spine straight, and hands relaxed. Become mindful of your breathing. Allow yourself to relax with each inhalation. As you allow your eyes to close gently, breathe out any tension you may be feeling. Gently and slowly now, scan your body for any area where you may be holding tension... scalp, face, neck, shoulders... breathe in relaxation, breathe out tightness. Move to your chest, stomach, arms, hands, and fingers... breathe deeply in and out. Your breathing is now deeper as you move to your legs, feet and toes... breathe out the last of your tiredness and tension. You are relaxed and focused on your breath.

You are walking on a path. You are relaxed, peaceful, and content. You are dressed comfortably and the temperature is just right, not too cold or too warm. You are enjoying being in nature. You can feel the warmth of the sun and a gentle breeze. You can hear the sweet chirping of birds. The fresh air tastes and smells clean and refreshing. As you walk along the path you begin to see a house ahead on the path. You decide to go to this house, and you understand somehow that this house has been waiting just for you. As you approach, notice the details of the outside of the house. Is it made of wood, brick, or stone? Is the house large or small? How many floors are there? How do the windows and doors appear? Notice the landscaping now. Is there a yard, flowers, trees? See these details just as you would like them to be.

Walk now to the front door. The door swings open just as you are ready to turn the knob. You are filled with the certainty that this house is for you, just for you. Step inside now and notice all the details of the interior. How is your house furnished? Are there many rooms or just a few? Are the rooms small and structured or large and open? Are there stairs? Where do they go? What colors, textures, objects do you see? Take time now to create and explore your house.

Pause

Now that you are well acquainted with your house, decide what you might like to do next. Feel free to read a book, listen to music, prepare a meal, make a cup of tea, write or paint, or do any relaxing activity that you enjoy. You know that whatever it is that you would like to do, your house has everything you could possibly need. Observe yourself now as you busy yourself with an activity that you enjoy.

Pause

Gently now, you realize that it is time to return to your path. Look around and memorize the details of your house. Understand that this house belongs to you, and that it will always be waiting for you anytime you wish, and it will always contain and provide exactly what you need. It's time to leave now, so close the door behind you and walk back to the path. As you walk for a few steps, you turn and look behind you. There you see your house in perfect detail. You know that you can return again and again whenever you wish. You turn now and resume your journey on the path.

You are relaxed, peaceful and content. You are breathing easily and deeply. Gently, begin to move your fingers and toes. You become aware of the chair in which you are sitting. Taking all the time you need, begin to stir and when you are ready, open your eyes.

Liz Bachtel is a holistic counselor from Westport, Massachusetts, who often uses guided imagery in her work. She is currently studying for her doctorate in Clinical Psychology.

32

Meeting the Shadow Self

Guide: Janet Doucette

"This is a very emotional and illuminating visualization."

Introduction

In workshops and groups I use this journey to get in touch with the "disinherited self." We work to make an ally of the shadow self and to learn how we use this part of personality in our lives. We see where and how we need to transform or heal certain aspects of it. The "shadow self" may take a great deal of processing, so it is not recommended as a frequent visualization. This meditation helps you look at aspects of yourself that you deny the most and to see yourself clearly.

The Journey

Begin with mindful breathing. Sit straight with your spine erect and hands placed gently on your thighs. As you breathe in allow the breath to spiral in, down, around, and through you nourishing your cells and organs. Relax and release the toxins and the tensions accumulated during the day. Release them out with the exhaled breath, out into the white light where they are absorbed. Sense your chakra energy centers opening one by one, spinning freely in a clockwise fashion.

You are walking down a hallway with many doors. Pause and look at each door carefully. Choose the door that beckons you. Notice its material, color, and the shape of doorknob. Open the door and walk down the stairway. Ten, nine, eight steps. Seven, six, five, four steps; three, two one step more. Now step onto a beautifully tiled, parquet floor.

Pause

Take a deep breath and then release it. Be mindful of your breathing, staying in the present, watching, accepting what comes to you. There is a mist gathering about you and you have the feelings of light, awareness, and joy. You may take time now to change your clothing or your appearance. When you are ready, step out from the cloak of mist.

Before you is the portal to your garden. Enter your medicine place and pay attention to the new things that have been growing here. Sit upon a bench or rock and breathe in fully the fine air. This garden is a great comfort to you, and it changes as we enter it again and again. You will be leaving to visit the Old One soon, and it is important that you connect fully with our Medicine Place. By the walkway or path at the edge of your garden is a gift for you. You must take this gift with you as we walk into the forest.

Pause

Prepare are now ready to walk into the dark forest. You are entering without guides, for now you know the way. Though the path is often dark, it is always safe for you. Walk quietly and purposely on this path. Soon you see a pale luminous light glowing in the clearing ahead. It is the place of the Old

One. But the clearing is empty. There is a fire burning in the center of the clearing but no one approaches. Sit down by the fire and feel its warmth.

Put your head down upon your knees and listen carefully for any sound that may come to you. Empty yourself of judgements, of attachments.

Pause

Soon you hear a rustling in the thicket and you raise your head. The Old One is sitting before you on a brightly colored blanket. His eyes gaze into yours with piercing intensity. Allow yourself to gaze back into his eyes, and let his energy fill you.

The Old One indicates that you are to stand and go with his messenger who is standing beside you right now, at the fire. You did not hear anyone approach, but there is indeed, someone standing beside you. This person is dressed in a long cloak and his face is hidden from you behind the fabric of a hood. Though this person is a stranger to you, you accept his direction and follow him into the woods.

The path is no more than a thin trail overgrown with thorns and thicket. The hooded figure takes you farther and farther into the woods. Ahead you see a thin, gray spire of smoke in the trees, and soon you come to a hide lodge which stands in the middle of a dense thicket.

The figure, who has not spoken to you in all this time, indicates that you should enter the lodge though it appears thick with smoke. You enter and sit upon fragrant cedar boughs. The figure enters the lodge and sits beside you. He holds out his hand to you. Place the gift you received in your garden in the palm of his hand....

Pause

Now the figure removes the hood and the shadowy figure's face becomes clear to you by the light of the fire. Recognize it now....

Pause

The figure asks you to heal him. The stranger asks how to be transformed. Listen to his words.

Pause

The gift you have placed in his hand has been altered, and the shadow warrior is returning this transformed gift to you. This is a symbol of your agreement with the shadow warrior. You will use this gift to heal the shadow in your life, to make it your ally. Though now, you are uneasy friends, you are agreeing to become allies in the future.

Now you must make your way back to the clearing of the Old One. The shadow will not accompany you. He will stay in the fire lodge in the thicket where you can visit when you have a need. It is not difficult to find the way back to the clearing, for the thicket is no obstacle to you.

Pause

You are standing again in the clearing of the Old One. The

fire is still burning brightly. There is an energy in the clearing, a feeling of power that is being shared with you. Sense this power, what it feels like, what color it is to you and where in your body it feels the most focused.

As you leave the clearing, you take some of that energy with you. You will bring it back into your garden. Walk along the forest path with confidence. The shadow warrior has been faced. You have traded gifts with the shadow and you have gained energy and focus in your life. This energy will rest in your garden until you are ready to use it.

When you reach the garden, find a place to put the energy that you received from the Old One. This energy does not have a name, it can only be felt, sensed. But you may choose a place in your garden for its safekeeping.

Pause

After you have done this and are ready to return to the circle — walk through the portal and change in the mist.

Welcome back.

Janet Ware Doucette uses guided imagery and cross-cultural healing techniques in workshops and support groups in order to enable others to experience their higher selves. A profound near-death experience in 1986 left her with an awareness of our abilities to heal ourselves.

33

Transformation

Guide: Loryn C. Martin

"Know and feel more than before, that God is within you."

Introduction

This imagery was created at a time in my life when it seemed every action ended in closed doors. I knew I needed to do intense inside work to get things flowing on a new level. Although I use the word "God" in this journey, it can be easily substituted with "Divine Presence." This meditation can facilitate your sincere desire to fully experience and feel God. I once practiced it for two hours, resulting in a tremendous transformation.

The Journey

Find a comfortable place to lie down, and as you do some slow deep breathing, feel yourself beginning to let go and surrender. As you inhale, visualize yourself inhaling light... as you exhale imagine you are letting go of all tensions and worries and allow yourself to totally surrender into the light. For this meditation is a meditation of surrendering to the light of God, the Divine Presence.

Visualize clouds above you and feel a sincere desire within you to allow the light of God to transform your life. As you do this the clouds above you begin to disperse and the light of the Great Central Sun begins to shine down upon you. Again, feel your desire for this light to transform you into a higher level of being. Feel the light entering you as you would feel the warmth of the sun on your skin. As you feel this light and visualize this light say to yourself over and over again, "The light of God is transforming my life now."

Pause

As you continue to visualize and feel this light permeating your being, say to yourself over and over again, "I open myself to receive and accept the transforming light, this Divine Presence, fully into my being and into every part of my life NOW."

Pause

Now shift your attention to feeling the light within your heart. Feel a gentle warmth there that permeates your whole being. Say to yourself as you feel this light, "I feel the presence of the light of God in my being now." Again, say it to yourself over and over again, visualizing a bright light shining in your heart.

Pause

Now as you feel this light in your heart, think of all the people in your life you care about and/or people who are sick or in need of more light in their lives. Feel and imagine this light is expanding and reaching out to them and ask in your heart that the light of God may also transform their life as it is yours.

Now allow this light to expand out throughout your home, your town, your state, your country, and throughout the earth herself and all the people on the earth, again asking that the light of God may transform all beings to a higher level.

Focus now on your first chakra and imagine this light moving into your chakra and say to yourself, "The light of God is now transforming this chakra to a higher level of being." Allow your focus to stay there for 10 seconds or more.

Pause

Repeat this same process with each of the main chakras.

Pause

Beginning again with the first chakra, repeat the same process with all seven chakras, two more times.

Pause

Say to yourself, "The light of God is transforming every level of my being now," as you visualize all seven chakras glowing brightly....

Pause

Focus once again, in your heart and think of all the things you have to be grateful for in your life and feel this gratefulness in your heart and say to yourself, "I am grateful to this Divine Presence in my life for all the good in my life." Still feeling the gratefulness in your heart, say to yourself, "I am grateful to the light for the transformation that has occurred in my being and may it allow me to truly realize the full presence of love and abundance that is in my life.

Loryn C. Martin is a teacher, therapist, healer, psychic, writer, and an artist from Colorado Springs, Colorado. She has been teaching and lecturing since she was 19 and has continued to do so over the past 15 years.

34

Twogathering

Guide: Christopher S. Rubel, Rel. D.

"This imagery is designed for self-simplifying and unites with the energy deep within."

Introduction

Too often, we gather around ourselves "complexifying" situations, things, people, and desires. In the midst of all that seems to pull on us, this way and that, we get lost as to who we are in our essence When one stays in the present, everything is simplified. Love and pro-active life become more available to you. I use this meditation with clients and myself to help decrease the power of what is projected, what is thrust into the personal shadow bag, and what takes on more importance than it deserves. Uniting opposites and reclaiming the shadow are essentials to feeling your humanness, your liveliness.

The setting for this journey should be free of distractions as much as possible. Find a place where you will not be self-conscious. People watching will think you are half a sandwich short of a picnic. They may think you're nuts. You might think so, too, but it works. Remember, it is what's going on inside that counts. If you find an argument about this, it is probably because of what is going on inside.

The Journey

(I like to begin by facing to the North.) Standing, breathe deeply, with your knees unlocked and your back straight. With each inhalation, stretch your arms above your head, and reach for the sky. With each exhale, let your arms down slowly, and let them hang limp by your sides. Your lungs are very empty. Also, with each exhalation, let your knees slightly bend. You don't want to be uncomfortable, but feel a slight tension in your knees as you bend them. Repeat this. Breathing in, stretch skyward. Breathing out, let your arms and knees come down, and feel earthward. Again, skyward, in; earthward, down and out. Repeat this eight to twelve times, feeling yourself become tired, wanting to let down, and gradually doing just that.

The Journey

Let yourself sink down, on a couch, a chair, or the floor. Let yourself become more and more relaxed and feel the tensions drain from your body and flow out of your muscles — all of your muscles — as your breathe in, slowly, and out, slowly, letting your body tingle and let go. As they release gathered tensions, you may find your muscles shaking just a bit from the standing.

Closing your eyes and letting go of all distractions, begin to let a safe, beautiful, (recalled or imaginary) place come to you. Let it materialize in your mind's eye. Begin to be there, wherever it is. Let it become real for you. The place itself, the surroundings, the time of day, the air, the life (animal, human, insect, etc.) that is around you. Let it all emerge and become increasingly real for you... a virtual reality. Let go of all distractions and detach from all stimuli. Like a train going by in the far distance, twigs floating by on a stream or birds flying across the horizon in the distance, all distractions come into your senses and then move through and out of your consciousness, leaving you freer and freer to go within. Let this process deepen throughout the guided meditation.

Let yourself begin to picture, first, to your right, a sunny landscape of yellows and blues; then, second, to your left, a darker place, a swamp at dusk or nighttime or a forest with a cave barely visible between the trees. Go back and forth, right to left, picturing the landscape and its brightness, then to your left, picturing the darkened swamp or forest. Let the images become more and more detailed as you look at them: right, left, then right, and so on.

Now, moving your awareness behind you, let yourself become aware of heat. Imagine a very, very warm, fire; the sun on a hot, tin roof; or a desert highway on an early August afternoon. Let yourself begin to feel the heat radiating from behind you. As the heat begins to become uncomfortable, move your awareness ahead of you, where there is freezing water, floating ice, or a barren, frozen tundra. Begin to feel the front of your body; notice your face and your hands becoming very, very cold. Let all the coldness gather.

Now move, right (light) to the sunny landscape; left (dark) to the darkened swamp; behind to the heat; and ahead to the coldness. Become familiar with a pattern of going slowly from right (light) to left (dark) and then back (hot) to front (cold). You will find you can do this, giving yourself time in each direction to gather the feelings and sensations of each direction. The internal east is sunlight, right brain, and receptivity. The internal west is left brain, darkness, complication, and foreboding, and it reminds you of the mysteries of the past. Ahead of you is the north—coldness, a polar and polarizing sensitivity. And behind you is the south, and its blistering heat. You begin to realize you are the center, the vortex, the convergence.

Pause

Gradually moving to high above you, let a rainbow of liquid feeling spill from a turning, spirit-water wheel and cascade over you and through you. It surrounds you, and you are able to move from feeling to feeling. Above you is a great waterwheel, slowly spilling its liquid feelings over you, bathing you. As each feeling washes over and through you, the next one begins to come from the next bucket of the wheel, splashing and washing over your nakedness. You are becoming freer of all that is not you. You are beginning to sense your essence, your simplicity.

The first feeling is one of curiosity and confusion. It washes over and through you. Let it soak in; feel it.

Pause

Then, the liquid of fear begins to wash over and through you. Let yourself feel fear, knowing there is another feeling on the way. Let it soak in and through you. And as it does, the next feeling of anger begins to wash over and through you. Let it soak in; tense your body, tighten your jaw just a bit, and feel the tension, the readiness of fight or flight. Let it soak in and through you.

Pause

As the "feelwheel" above you turns, spilling over and through you, begin to let go, releasing, and relaxing. Let this continue to happen until you feel lighter and clearer, almost translucent. Gradually, let your body feel peaceful, safe, and free from the chains of any tensions. Let this spiritual sense soak in, gracefully, peacefully.

Pause

Smoothly, move into the solar plexus. Imagine that area of your body and begin to let all of your awareness gather there as if you are filling a chalice. As the chalice fills, it begins to spill over with the healing, grace-light liquid. It flows up through your spine, and you feel yourself in a new present, a new moment. There is nothing dividing you, at this moment. You are a unit, a fresh child, a wholeness. You are participating more fully in the now. Being here now, you are free of all divisions, all opposites, and this unitary awareness is empowering and refreshing. There is nothing complicated in your consciousness, now. You are closer to your essence, your knowledge of your unique soul-nature, than you have ever been. This is the place-time for healing, for clarity, and for a centered peace that will help empty the bag of all of its collected shadow elements. They are all absorbed, now, in the wholeness of who you are. You know yourself to be loved, now, in your simplicity.

As you reach that deepest place of this union of all opposites and the absorption of all that complicates your life, you begin to hear your name.

Pause

Listen to your name, called affectionately, as an invitation. You want to say, "Yes." Your name comes three times in this awareness place. Gently, you hear your name and begin to move slowly into present clock time.

Ascend slowly from this very deep place, moving up slowly with the bubbles, no faster. Move from ten fathoms, nine fathoms, eight fathoms, seven fathoms, six fathoms, five fathoms, four fathoms. Pause there, feeling your strength, becoming more aware your body and your muscles. Move to three fathoms, two fathoms. You are almost to the top now. Feel energized and very at home with what is about to be available to you, the opportunities that await you. You come to the surface and find yourself in your safe place. You may return here at any time you wish to just breathe in and out. All you need to do to reach this place more and more easily is to practice the breathing, the relaxing, and let this experience continue to build in power and effectiveness.

Thank you for sharing this unifying experience. You have done well with this. It will flow more easily each time. You will enjoy it more each time and find new images in each direction as the spiritual dimensions of this imagery increase for you.

Christopher S. Rubel, Rel. D., is an Episcopal priest as well as a licensed Marriage, Family, and Child Therapist, in private practice in Claremont, California. He has been practicing for more than twenty-five years, moving through many modalities of therapy. His current work with Jungian methods, hypnosis, and imagery have added a new zest to his life and work. His special interests include Post Traumatic Stress and working with people to overcome inner "splits" and the reclaiming of personal and projected "shadows."

Self-Esteem

35

Animal Meditation

Guide: Margot Escott, M.S.W.

"Positive results of this imagery is enhancement of self-esteem."

Introduction

Inspiration for this journey came from my early teachers in visualization and body-work, particularly Ilana Rubenfeld and Moshe Feldenkris. Our alienation from the natural world is resulting in disastrous efforts on all the other living beings on our planet. By connecting with other animals, I believe that we are enhancing our potential to truly be spiritual beings in a material world.

Playing environmental music — sounds of the rain forest, the beach — or any of the Goldens Voyage tapes, may enhance your ability to evoke creative images on this journey. When I do this imagery at workshops, I have large drawing paper and colorful markers available to participants and encourage them to draw what they experienced on this trip as soon as they come back to waking consciousness. You may also become aware that the qualities which drew you to the animal are qualities that you, too, possess. If you don't see these particular qualities in yourself, ask a close friend what he or she sees — you may be surprised. Others often see us quite differently than we see ourselves. By identifying the positive attributes of your animal, you have chosen those qualities in yourself, some of which you are not able to see quite yet.

This imagery may be done with children or in a family setting.

The Journey

Start to relax by taking a few deep abdominal breaths. As you inhale, say to yourself, "I am" and on the exhale say, "at peace." Continue this mantra for several breaths... then allow your breathing to become easy and natural.

Let your conscious mind, full of thoughts and plans, take a vacation and allow your unconscious mind to take over. The unconscious mind is that reservoir of all knowledge and is the part that connects us with every living being on our planet.

As you drift deeper into a pleasant state of relaxation, let go of any thoughts concerning anything other than peace and serenity.

See yourself in a beautiful place in nature. This can be any setting that feels comfortable and safe to you. As you walk through this place, you feel at one with your body and the universe. You note that you walk effortlessly and easily through this environment. Begin to explore this place with all of your senses. See the types of foliage and notice the colors are the plants and flowers? If you are near water, what color is the water? Be aware of any patterns that are displayed in this special place for you. Since this is your personal journey, you can combine anything from favorite places that you have actually visited as well as images that you have only seen in pictures or read about. Be aware of the different textures that surround you. Feel objects that are smooth or rough... use all your senses. Feel the breezes as they gently envelope your body.

Now you hear in the distance the sounds of many different animals. You see that you are in a garden of all kinds of creatures — every type of animal that you want to imagine is here. Since this is a special, magical place, all of these animals are safe and loving towards you. You are able to touch all of the animals be aware of the different textures of their bodies. What kinds of feelings do you get by touching, holding, and being with these special animals. Be aware of the wonderful smells of these animals—let yourself immerse all of your senses in this scene.

You become aware of being drawn to one particular animal. If this creature is small, you may hold it in your hands, if it is large, you may want to ride on it. Know that this animal is safe and begin to explore the world accompanied by this animal. Notice the view of the world that this animal has— see the world from this special place. As you spend time with this animal — running, flying, swimming, leaping — be aware of the essence of your animal. What qualities drew you to her? What made this animal so special to you? Spend the next few moments truly being with this creature.

Pause

When you are ready to leave this place and your special friend, know that you can return at any time. Just close your eyes, breathe some relaxing breaths, and let your imagination take you to your special place.

36

Garden of the Heart

Guide: Nancy Carlton

"Heal the pain of feelings such as loneliness, self-doubt and rejection."

Introduction

This imagery can be used for healing old parental wounds and new pain. It helps the listener to accept pain and teaches ways to work through it. It also creates important feelings of security, dissipating feelings of isolation and loneliness often associated with painful situations.

The Journey

Sit or lie down in a relaxed and comfortable position. Close your eyes and start breathing slowly and deeply from your abdomen, relaxing more and more with each breath. Your breathing comes easily and naturally as your join the rhythm of the universe.

Pause

Imagine you are walking on a path through a forest of lush greenery. The trees surrounding you make you feel protected and peaceful. Even though you know you have a destination, you are exactly where you are supposed to be. As you inhale, you breathe deeply the woody scents around you, feeling alive and well. You feel the crunch of wood and leaves beneath your feet. You listen to the sounds of the forest: squirrels rustling, birds singing, bees buzzing, little furry animals chattering, and you become one with it. This is where you belong.

Pause

Tucked away, almost hidden among the trees, you see a door that you know is there just for you. You walk to the door, open it, and find a hall of stairs going down. You start walking down the stairs and with each step you become more and more relaxed.

Pause

At the bottom of the stairs is an opening that leads into a garden, your garden. Take time now to stand in the doorway enjoying the loveliness of your special garden.

Pause

On a bench in the middle of your garden a man and woman are waiting for you. They are eternally young and beautiful, perfect in their infinite knowledge and loving gentleness. They are your universal parents. The Mother and Father who are here to answer your questions, listen to your fears and tears, hold you when you are lonely, and share your pain with you. Their love and compassion and support for you and help you cope with these painful feelings.

Sit down on the ground in front of them, place your head on

your Mother's lap and receive her nurturing love and tenderness. To your parents you are pure and infinite goodness. They are not here to judge you, but to love you. They are tender and gentle and warm loving with your feelings. You are the most special person in their lives. They are here to comfort you and guide you. Ask whatever questions you wish, know the answers you receive will help to heal you.

Pause

When you are ready, slowly bring yourself back to your present surroundings by first being aware of your breathing. Open your eyes to the present, still feeling the sense of peace and love you acquired while in your garden.

Nancy Alexandre who resides in Naples, Florida, calls herself "a student of life," and has worked in numerous areas of the service industry.

37

Self-Esteem Enrichment

Guide: Rodney L. Goulet, C.Ht.

"For those who feel uncertain of their origin, of their self worth and purpose."

Introduction

This meditation is based upon the teachings found in the "Course of Miracles," published by the Foundation for Inner Peace, Tiburon, California.

You are about to enjoy a very pleasant experience. Assume a comfortable position. You may sit or lie down as you choose. The only requirement is to feel unrestricted... let all you muscles be at rest.

The Journey

Take a deep breath... hold it now... one, two... let it out now... all the way... let it all out now. Take another deep breath... hold it now... one, two, three... let it out now... all the way... let it all out now... all, all, all. Take yet another deep breath... hold it now... one, two, three, four... let it out now... all the way... let it all out now... all of it... all... all.... Now just relax... floating, hearing a soft sound far off... you are getting closer, closer now, hearing the sound of the ocean, you are now hearing the peaceful... restful... serene sounds of the ocean. The waves are moving... moving to the shore.... Imagine a relaxing wave... is moving through you now... relaxing... and quieting... every muscle... and nerve in your body. You are breathing... easily now.... Let your body have all the room it needs to relax and let go as you move now to a quiet place within.... This quiet place within... what you are experiencing is "that place where the small, still voice resides.

Just as the waves move now toward the shore... let a wave of relaxation move gently up through your legs... through your thighs... through your abdomen... just let go, relax and enjoy. The wave moves up now... up... up... through your body... relaxing every muscle and nerve.... Let go... let all your muscles relax....

Imagine now... the waves... as they move in toward the shore... the swell breaking... and freeing the energy of the ocean... as each wave reaches the sand and crashes... you feel the energy and tension releasing from your body... and let go now... and feel peace move into and through your body and your mind.

You hear the seagulls calling as they float by... drifting and floating, easily... as they soar into the distance... as you float easily into relaxation... as you feel peaceful now.

Your thoughts now drift through slowly... slowly... slowly.... You now gently... push them away, push them away... as you listen to the sounds of the ocean... you are so relaxed... your body floats, easily, as you hear the sounds of the ocean, gently... floating... easily.... Your body feels weightless... just floating... the thoughts now have drifted past... just as the seagulls... gently glide past... gently move out of your vision... easily gone from your mind.

You now are in this place... this peaceful... restful... place, where you now hear a small, still, quiet voice... gently, peacefully... urging you to listen... listen now... listen to this voice... this loving voice.... The voice is speaking to you... this loving voice is whispering softly... listen to the thoughts... loving you... teaching love....

You hear the words, "You are goodness, you are a manifestation of My divine love on this planet. I brought you here in this time to love, to be loved, to teach love to others. I can only create perfection, so you are perfect as you are. It is not necessary for you to know anything else to experience your birthright, which is wholeness. You are a part of Me; you have never been away from Me. Your future is assured. You have nothing missing; you are complete as you are, and you need none other than Me. When you need to know what path to follow, return to the quiet and listen, I will show you the way. Rest now, assured that you are perfect just as you are. Love yourself, love others, teach love."

You are now slowly... easily... gently... returning to awareness of the room about you... opening your eyes... feeling wonderful... rested... relaxed... move your arms... stretch easily... take a deep breath... and gently let it all out.

Rodney L. Goulet is a certified hypnotherapist who studied under Gil Boyne at the Los Angeles School of Hypnosis in 1988. His specialties include increasing confidence in performers and weight control. Goulet was born in 1933 in Minneapolis, Minnesota, and attended St. Thomas College in St. Paul, Minnesota. He currently lives in Oceanside, California.

Training & Skill

38

30 Second Self-Hypnosis

Guide: Roger Bernhardt, Ph.D.

Introduction

Repeat the following exercise as often as you wish, whether once a day or once every couple of hours.

The Journey

Begin by making yourself as comfortable as you can. Your feet should rest side by side and uncrossed, a few inches apart. Your arms should lie in repose.

Roll your eyes up toward your eyebrows, as high as you can get them. Try to see the top of your head. With your eyes still gazing upward, slowly close your eyelids and, at the same time, take a deep breath. Exhale. Let your eyes relax. Let your body float down.

It's a very pleasant feeling. Now, while in this comfortable state, indulge yourself. In your mind's eye, picture yourself in a place where you have been or would like to go, some spot where you can be perfectly at ease and at peace with yourself and the world.

As you picture yourself at the pleasant site of your own choosing, you continue to float down. Your body is almost a thing apart from you now. You can leave it in place and remove yourself slightly from it. You can now give your body instructions as to how you want it to live.

In the blank space below insert whatever thinking, feeling or act you aim to overcome, e.g. sad thoughts, fear, anger, smoking, difficulty going to sleep.... Then say to yourself:

"For my body, not for me but for my body, ________________ is a poison... I need my body to live... To the degree I want to live, I will protect my body."

Picture yourself as you would like to be: strong, confident, self-assured, at ease with yourself and the world around you. You feel calm and comfortable and filled with a sense of self-satisfaction for becoming master over your body rather than the reverse.

You are now ready to emerge from your self-hypnosis, to do so, count silently backward from three to one: Three. Get ready. Two. With your eyelids still closed, roll your eyes upward. One. Let your eyelids slowly open. Now, make tight fists with your hands, then, spread your fingers wide and simultaneously yawn.

Dr. Roger Bernhardt, now retired and living in Naples, Florida, was a psychoanalyst and hypnotherapist based in New York City. He served as chief psychologist at New Jersey State Hospital and a staff psychologist at the Veterans Administration Hospital in Buffalo, New York. He has lectured at several universities across the country.

39

Bedwetting

Guides: Larry and Lucas Moen

"I have used this imagery with my son who showed remarkable results."

Introduction

The success of this guided imagery is due in part to the language. Often a parent or guardian is aware of the importance of positive strokes but may not always use them. The child is entitled to hear these words even if they do not always come easily. Aside from this, it is equally successful because of the one-on-one attention you give your child. You are focused one hundred percent on your child and that alone says you love, care, and are willing to help him or her through a difficult time.

More than three million children are bedwetters. After age four concern should be given to a possible disorder. Low self-esteem, shame, guilt, or embarrassment are feelings often associated with a bedwetter. Although children usually outgrow this disorder by their mid-teens, I believe the process can be expedited by using the following imagery.

We recommend you read this journey after all bedtime hygiene needs have been met—face washed, teeth brushed, bladder emptied, all goodnights said and everyone settled down for bed.

The Journey

Lie flat on your back with your arms and legs uncrossed; place your arms along the sides of your body, close your eyes, and relax your entire body. Imagine a space shuttle on a launch pad. When the spaceship takes off, you will be completely relaxed. Inhale very deeply; 6... 5... exhale... 4... 3... inhale... 2... 1... exhale ... Blast Off! You are one relaxed munchkin.

Visualize a movie screen—a big white screen. On this screen, see yourself lying in bed just as you are now. Notice every detail of yourself and your bed. Look at your clothes, and see how dry they are. See clearly the dry pillowcases, dry sheets, and dry bedspread or blanket. See how dry everything is and notice how warm and cozy you are.

Now visualize yourself moving into the future and sleeping this entire evening. You wake up tomorrow morning just the way you are now relaxed, accepting, loved, and dry. You did not wet the bed. You are dry just as you are now. Your sheets, pillowcases, and clothing are dry. You have a beautiful relaxed expression on your face. How pleased you are because of your successful dry night. You are maturing beautifully.

People in other parts of the house sense you have had a dry night and happily begin to enter your room. Fifteen people you know are standing all around your bed. More are coming. Now thirty are standing in rows of two. They all smile and look at you with praise for a wonderful completely dry night while sleeping. Thirty more people file through the door. Now there are sixty people in your room — some of them standing on their toes just to get a glimpse of you. Now, two adults put their hands gently under you and lift you off the bed and onto their shoulders. As you press your way through the crowd, you notice the entire house filled with party people. A woman stops you and puts a party hat on your head. There are more people outside looking in through the windows, pressing their noses against the glass to see you.

You are a special person who has accomplished the marvelous goal of being dry. The front door bursts open, and there is a crowd lining your sidewalk yelling, jumping, and waving. Hundreds of spectators are there to welcome you. There are three fire trucks with sirens blaring and lights flashing, a big cement truck; a tractor pulling a wagon of Hershey Bars; girls, lots of girls; and lots of boys; money flying through the air, flying everywhere; the Kansas City football team; and every member of the Chicago Bears football team. There are lots of animals, camels, mice , rats, dogs, cats, birds, lions, tigers, snakes, beavers, turtles, platypus, cheetahs, elephants, zebras, storks, egrets, flamingos, penguins, and alligators. Your most feared bedroom monsters have their arms around each other and are smiling and dancing. Ferraris and Lamborghinis are yours if you want them. Fireworks are shooting off in all directions. The crowd carries you to a huge dry bed on a blue wagon being pushed by two leprechauns. A hydraulic lift raises the bed fifty feet in the air, and the parade continues. By this time there are thousands of spectators jammed on your street with balloons and music, free coke, and free popcorn. Free everything.

The crowd is overwhelmed with joy and cheers, "Hail to the Dryness King, the King of Dry, the Wonderful King of

Dryness." The parade continues for twenty-nine hours, and then ends on the thirtieth hour. You show everyone your wonderful loving quality by thanking them for coming. Everyone cleans up the mess except you. You are lowered down to street level, free to return home and go quietly to bed.

If you wake up wet, that's okay. We all make mistakes, and you are certainly entitled to waking up either dry or wet; that is your choice.

You are capable of accomplishing an entire evening of light sleep, dry and safe. Deep, heavy sleep isn't necessary because you are no longer frightened. You are healthy, lovable, and loved, and waking up dry will be your reality. You have an abundance of self-confidence, and you are fearless when sleeping at night, you are strong and secure. You are also secure in your surroundings. You are secure with your bed, what is under your bed, with the furniture, with the room itself, with the closet and its contents, and with everything outside the room. Everything in the rest of the house, outside and around the house, the roof, and everything in your entire neighborhood is safe and secure.

You are now free to sleep knowing that you will awaken in the morning dry and comfortable just as you are now. You realize that your mother loves you, your father loves you, everyone you contact loves you. So drift off to sleepy-timeland and wake up tomorrow morning refreshed and dry. And know that I love you.

40

Image Streaming

Guide: Tom Kenyon

"Research has indicated that Image Streaming can increase analytical abilities and other intelligence factors."

Introduction

In this exercise you will be using something called "the inner witness." This "inner witness" is a function of the higher cortical centers in your brain. The "witness" allows you to be aware of yourself experiencing an event, not just experiencing an event, but aware of yourself experiencing the event.

It may seem odd, at first, to describe outloud your experiences, but it is the process of description that increases your intelligence in this exercise. The tape will evoke many different types of experiences such as fantasies, visual images, physical sensations, memories, etc. Normally, we do not describe these types of things. But by describing every detail of your inner experience, you will be making linkages between the language part of your brain with other areas. This linkage facilitates an increase in verbal abilities as well as intelligence.

This process is greatly facilitated through the use of music. Either New Age type compositions or the largo Movements of baroque music are very helpful. Play music at low volume in the background to help generate impressions that can, in turn, be verbalized.

Exercise

Sit comfortably with your eyes closed. You will start the process by doing something called Level One Breathing. This breathing pattern "slows down" your brain waves with an increase in mental imagery.

Level One Breathing

1. Inhale to a count of 8 (each count about one second)
2. Hold the breath in to a count of 8
3. Exhale to a count of 8
4. Hold the breath out to a count of 8
5. Repeat the above sequence 7 more times for a total of 8

The Journey

Begin to describe in minute detail the most subtle impressions, be they visual images, feelings, sensations, memories or fantasies. The more detailed your description the more effective this process will be. If you think you are not experiencing anything describe your "blank" in detail. This will eventually open up some kind of impression that you can then describe. It is the verbal description in your mind that makes this technique work. Some people may find that talking into an imaginary tape recorder helps.

The technique of Image Streaming was developed by Win Wenger, Ph.D., to dramatically increase certain intelligence factors such as verbal and analytical abilities as well as creativity. Persons interested in contacting Dr. Wenger directly may do so by writing Dr. Win Wenger, Project Renaissance, Box 332, Gaithersburg, MD 20884-0332. Copies of Research abstracts demonstrating the effectiveness of the Image Streaming technique may be procured by writing Quantum Link, 8665 Miami River Rd., Cincinnati, Ohio 45247. Ask for the Imager Streaming Research Bulletin.

Tom Kenyon, M.A. holds a master's degree in psychological counseling from Columbia Pacific University and has a private psychotherapy practice in Chapel Hill, North Carolina. He is also the founder and director of research and development for ABR, Inc. (Acoustic Brain Research) a leader in psychoacoustic research. Psychoacoustics is the study of how sound, language and music affect the brain and human behavior. He is also the originator of Body/Mind Re-education™ a form of rapid transformation used by therapists and counselors. Mr. Kenyon conducts human potential training in both the United States and Asia.

41

Peaceful Workplace

Guide: Marjorie Michael Munly

"You can create positive associations with your job and place of work."

Introduction

This meditation was inspired by my realization that people often lack positive associations with their occupations and places of work. They often feel hurried, overwhelmed, and out of touch with their hearts' desires. With this imagery, you can create a peaceful association with your workplace and enliven the realms of possibilities regarding your work experiences. This visualization can be used each evening before bedtime for two weeks, after which time you can taper off as your awareness of your job shifts. It is also beneficial to record the experiences that may surface while using this imagery.

The Journey

Begin as usual by assuming a comfortable position, taking several slow, deep breaths in through the nose and out through the mouth.

Next allow your attention to go to each area of your body,

beginning with your feet. Feel each bone, muscle, and joint become very heavy. Your mind and body easily let go of any effort or tension.

Pause

It is morning. You look out the window and see a perfectly blue sky. A gentle breeze accompanies the distant singing of birds. You have a strong sense that today will be refreshing and uplifting — perhaps even magical.

You are especially relaxed and unhurried while getting ready for work. What a joy to have an abundance of time to get ready for work! It feels so good to relax. Travel to work is effortless. Traffic flows quickly and green lights are in abundance. Pedestrians and motorists look happy. Smiling comes naturally. As you enter your workplace, you sense an exquisite level of comfort. There is a very apparent feeling of warmth, harmony, and pleasure here. Co-workers greet you openly and are eager to support you. They are positive and full of energy. Your work space looks changed and beautiful. You remember — last week it was renovated upon your request. All is now complete.... What was it you wanted?... A larger space?... Your favorite works of art on the walls?... New carpeting?... beautiful plants?... skylights?... The sky is the limit. Use your imagination.

Pause

It's lunch time. You are surprised that a close friend has brought you your favorite lunch—complete with a beautiful bouquet of flowers. You enjoy it together peacefully on the lawn outside your place of work. Had you noticed the embellished landscaping?

Pause

Your afternoon is equally pleasant. A deep sense of joy and fulfillment underlies all your tasks and interactions. Time passes ever so quickly. It is time to leave before you know it. You continue to feel very light and full of energy. On the way home, the thought occurs to you, "Could tomorrow be this good?" You know the answer... yes! The abundance of peace, joy, and beauty experienced today are mere reflections of your true nature.

Marjorie Michael Munly, who lives in Arlington, Virginia, is an early childhood educator and a pioneer of peace and awareness education in the public schools (for staff and students). She has been a teacher of meditation for twenty years.

42

Visualization Development

Guide: Tom Kenyon

"Developing the ability to visualize is a very gratifying experience. It deepens and enriches one's inner world."

Introduction

Research has indicated that all people (except for the blind) process visual information whether they have access to internal visual images or not. For many persons this information is also processed consciously. These are the "good visualizers." They can "see" in their "mind's eye" real or imagined objects and scenes. With more advanced visualization abilities a person can actually rotate an imaginary object in space and "see" aspects that were hidden from the front view. The famed scientist Nikolai Tesla had this remarkable ability.

It is possible for almost any person to develop and/or increase their visualization abilities. It is important to remember that you already visualize. You may simply not realize this, or you may not be able to access this ability consciously.

The following protocol, if used faithfully, will develop your visualization abilities and if you already visualize, it will greatly increase your abilities.

Ideally this exercise should be practiced for about twenty minutes a day. It may take a few days or a few weeks to develop your visualization abilities. Most "non-visualizing" people require several attempts at this exercise before they start to "see" internal visual images. Be patient and have fun with this exercise. If you already have the ability to visualize, this method can enhance that ability.

The Journey

Find a color picture, preferably one that captures your imagination. Place the picture in front of you and as you look at the picture describe to yourself, in minute detail, every thing about the picture as you look at it.

What are the colors, shapes? Take a good five minutes to look at and verbally describe every detail. The more details you notice and describe, the more effective the exercise will be.

After you have completed this part of the exercise, close your eyes. Now imagine the picture in front of you, and begin to describe what you "see" in your "mind's eye." If it seems that you do not "see" anything, repeat your earlier verbal description (when your eyes were opened). As you go through your description you may begin to sense subtle visual impressions, as if you can almost "see" in your imagination what you are describing to yourself.

After you have worked with re-creating a visual image of the picture in your "mind's eye", begin to imagine that the picture is a 3-D image. Imagine yourself moving through this three dimension landscape. Feel and sense what this would be like. Imagine looking at the objects from different angles and directions. It may help to verbally describe these imaginary experiences to yourself as you move through the 3-D landscape.

Tom Kenyon, M.A. holds a master's degree in psychological counseling from Columbia Pacific University and has a private psychotherapy practice in Chapel Hill, North Carolina. He is also the founder and director of research and development for ABR, Inc. (Acoustic Brain Research) a leader in psychoacoustic research. Psychoacoustics is the study of how sound, language and music affect the brain and human behavior. He is also the originator of Body/Mind Re-education™ a form of rapid transformation used by therapists and counselors. Mr. Kenyon conducts human potential training in both the United States and Asia.

Freedom & Awareness

43

Become the Eagle

Guide: Nancy Harn-Wagner

"Learning to listen to the animals as they speak, has prompted me to write this visualization."

Introduction

This powerful visualization encourages you to take on the strength of the highest flying bird and allows you to see what your part might be in the healing of the earth. "Become the Eagle" can also open the mind to its potential and help you discover your purpose in life.

The Journey

Close your eyes and lift yourself into the clouds; rise high above the earth and know that you can observe like the eagle.

As you begin your flight, take long deep breaths of air into your lungs — rhythmically sensing the clearness of the air so high above the earth.

Pause

Allow yourself to float blissfully as you take in the quiet stillness above. Notice how peaceful it is to hear only the gentle winds that assist you in your flight.

See the white light of protection coming from the center of your body, filling your entire body and spreading out through your wings to the sky about you. Soar peacefully as you quiet all your thoughts and revel in this transformation.

Becoming the eagle takes on great responsibility for the eagle is one who flies the highest of all birds and carries the greatest stick. You begin to sense your obligation and why you have been chosen to become this bird.

You will notice your eyesight has become very keen and your wings unbelievably strong. Realizing you had been given an enormous amount of inner strength, you feel as though you could do anything you wished — or become anything you desired — or accomplish any task or change you wanted. Breathe in this ability and know it is yours.

What a glorious capability to have this vigor, this inner spirit... think of the powerful effect you could have on the universe.

And so now — what is your plan? Think for a few minutes about what you want to accomplish with this new talent you have been given.

Do you want to teach others? Do you want to write or speak? Is it your desire to have an important role in healing the earth? Gather your thoughts and at the end of this visualization write down your ideas on what you want to accomplish in your life.

This is a beautiful time for you — a step you have wanted to take, an answer you have asked for. Be thankful. Take on the spirit of the eagle and fly in any direction you wish.

As you return from your flight give thanks to the Eagle Spirit. Open your eyes when you are ready.

Nancy Harn-Wagner professional visionary artist and writer who resides in Clearwater, Florida.

44

Dolphin

Guide: Chrystle Clae

"This meditation was inspired by a very special dolphin."

Introduction

The dolphin that inspired this journey is blind in one eye, but he is a wonderful ambassador of his species who welcomes visitors — especially children. This imagery helps create balance and peace of spirit eventually connecting you with your sense of oneness with all. Teenagers who use this meditation at night, have found it helps them become relaxed for sleep.

The Journey

Use any method of relaxation you like best, together with a couple minutes of deep breathing.

Pause

With your mind's eye, imagine you are lying on a warm sandy beach. The ocean water is calm and crystal clear. Go up to the shore and slowly wade into the water until it's up to your shoulders. You can see the sand and shells by your feet.

As you might have guessed, this is magical water. This is the kind of water in which you can breathe. There are no dangers in this protected, special place.

Quietly, a gentle dolphin glides by you. She swims a little farther out and begins to playfully leap and arch in the ocean water, hardly making any splash as she re-enters and slowly swims beside you. This time she rolls over slightly to look at you. You know that she is telepathically telling you to hold onto her dorsal fin and go for a ride.

The flesh of the dolphin is soft and sweet feeling, like a baby's cheek. As a result of your decision to trust your friend, you are treated to the ability of viewing other dimensions of reality.

Safe in the embrace of your dolphin, you begin viewing the earth you live in with different eyes. Pictures of forests are before your eyes. Look closely, you can see the light of life glowing from within and without the plant life of the forest. Even the rocks are alive with an energy of their own. The streams and rivers have a visible spirit. Relax and observe all the different forms of earth life that appear to you in this extrasensory way of experiencing them.

Pause

Comfortable and at ease, you find yourself swimming once more with your smiling friend. Your dolphin telepathically tells you it's time for her to swim out to deeper sea, but you can be with her anytime you choose in that other dimension of reality just by remembering the feel of her skin and the love that she radiates to you.

Walk out of the water onto the sandy beach. Your body feels

much heavier as you walk on shore. It's a different feeling, but it feels good to be grounded. Sense the vibration through the bottom of your feet. It's the heartbeat of Mother Earth. Take another moment and let that vibration soothe your body from the bottom of your toes to the top of your head. Taking a slow, deep breath open your eyes whenever you feel comfortable and ready.

Chrystle Clae is an astrologer, psychic counselor, and teacher in Seminole, Florida. She is a nationally-known writer on the subject of metaphysics and she has a column for psychic advice in the "Suncoast Beach Reporter." She is listed in "Who's Who in Service to the Earth."

45

Flowing

Guide: Jean D. Stouffer

"Learn to let go of things beyond your control and be willing to 'go with the flow.'"

Introduction

Life has highs and lows, harsh times and gentle times. This meditation, through its images, helps the listener to see and feel that the turbulence of the waterfalls and the swirl of the whirlpools are temporary; quiet times inevitably follow. "Flowing" creates the atmosphere to learn about letting go of situations beyond one's control and to accept the transitory nature of all things in life. This imagery can be used for relaxation before sleep or for creating quiet times during the day.

The Journey

As you take a deep breath and then another, you feel your body begin to relax, to let go... to let go of the tensions that may have built up. You can let the tension drain out of your eyelids and allow your eyes to close. And you allow that relaxing to spread slowly and comfortably throughout your body, allowing each muscle to become more and more relaxed. You can even wonder how relaxed you can become, as you focus on the comfortable feelings in your body. It feels so good to let go and be comfortable.

And as you continue to breathe in and out, letting go and relaxing even more with each breath, you allow yourself to travel to a lovely stream. You can see the stream now, and the tall canopy of trees overhead. Notice the shadows of the leaves dancing on the water. Hear the gentle sound of the water as it gurgles over the rocks. Birds are singing and the breeze is soft upon your face as you gaze into the water. The warm smells of summer surround you.

And as you watch the water, you might notice a leaf floating by. Is it a maple leaf? A cottonwood leaf? What kind of leaf is it? And as you watch, you can wonder about the leaf. Maybe you can even be the leaf. What would it be like to ride down a stream, sometimes swirling and eddying, sometimes drifting in calm waters, sometimes tumbling over small or large waterfalls.

And now you are the leaf, drifting and floating. You realize you can find out many things by being a leaf. You can swirl in a pool of water, spinning and twirling. You can hear a waterfall ahead. You can even anticipate the turbulence. Yet, you can ride the waterfall, tumbling and tossing in the frothing water. And as you do, you understand something. For every swirl and for every waterfall, there is a quiet time that follows, a quiet time of drifting and floating. This is so in all of life. And you can have this knowing in every cell of your being. You can have this knowing now. Take some time to really feel this knowing, to let it become a part of you. Take as much time as you wish.

Pause

And when you are ready, you can bid your stream good-bye, knowing that you can return to it any time you wish, to be the leaf again, to drift and float down the stream. And as you wonder what this new knowledge will mean to you, you can begin to shift just a little. You can shift comfortably into the here and now, in your own time, at your own pace.

Jean D. Stouffer is a writer and a certified hypnotherapist (American Council of Hypnotist Examiners and Southwest Hypnotherapists Examining Board) currently living in Albuquerque, New Mexico.

46

Forest Pool

Guide: Jack Kern

"Feel a way of letting go of old states in order take on new directions."

Introduction

This guided visualization is beneficial for releasing old emotions and conditions of the mind and body. It gives one a feeling of renewal and newness. Relax and make sure your body is comfortable and willing to let go of anything that stands between you and your Lord.

Take a deep breath and let it out. Let your breathing resume its normal rhythm but remember that feeling of letting go of your breath. Remember that as you let go of your breath, you let loose of old memories, hurts, fears, bitterness, and all those things that you no longer need and you no longer serve. You let go of them just as easily as you let go of your breath. Each time you breathe out, be conscious that you're not only releasing tension from your physical body, but you're also letting go of anything that no longer serves you and anything that stands in the way of the full realization of who and what you are, and who and what your Lord is in you. Each time you breathe in, each time you take in a breath, in your imagination know that your are breathing in life, energy, and spirit and that you are gradually filled to greater and greater degree as you empty yourself of the old stuff and the old tensions and even the physical discomfort of pain. As you breathe in, you draw in all that you need.

On this journey, you may bring along anyone you feel is in need of healing, guidance, or some other need. Let him or her come along but let him have his own experiences.

The Journey

Imagine that you are walking through a forest that has the deep stillness that you often find in a forest. Maybe there's a breeze sighing on the top of the trees, but on the forest floor it is quiet, and you walk along and feel the softness of the earth and the pine needles beneath your feet, and you smell the pine and the fragrance of flowers. Thoroughly tune in to the quiet and the sense of wonder, the sense of peace, that is here in the forest. Continue to walk through this forest until you come to a pool in the middle of the forest.

It's a small pool, formed by a waterfall and a small stream. There is a gentle waterfall coming down the hillside splashing over the rocks into the pool. The pool is very quiet, very still, very inviting. You put your toe in the pool, and it's not cold as you expected, but is the perfect temperature. You can't resist going into the pool, so you take off your clothes and fold them and lay them aside on one of the rocks. You slip gently into the pool. It's deep enough so you can go right up to your neck; you can go under the water if you wish. You feel the wetness and the coolness of the water; you feel how it supports you; you feel the gentle fall of the water on the rocks from that little waterfall. You find yourself completely at ease, perfectly supported, perfectly secure.

Then allow something to happen in this pool. Allow yourself, your body, to melt into the water so that you become one with the water. You even allow yourself to go under the water. You put your head completely under, and you find you have no problem breathing; there is no fear. You feel the sense of oneness with all that is around you in this pool. You feel as if your body has completely dissolved, yet there is nothing to be afraid of. It feels right. You allow every cell of your body to be cleansed and refreshed and reviewed in this pool — every cell washed clean and then gently reformed into God's perfect idea of what your body should be. Gently you feel your body reforming, coming back together out of the pool of water. Bring your head up above the water, and you look at the sky and the sunlight coming down through the trees. You are very happy to be there and to be alive and feeling so wonderfully refreshed.

You sit on a rock just under the waterfall, and you let it fall over your face and hair. Let it fall down over your body completely and enjoy your renewed sense of being cleansed and refreshed. You are a new creature whose old patterns and old habits and ways of looking at yourself have been washed away. And when you have enjoyed the waterfall long enough step out of the pool into the sunlight in the clearing. Let your skin and hair dry; go back to where you left your clothes and find that your clothes are different from the ones you left there. You try them on, and they fit perfectly. They feel beautiful, and you look and feel wonderful in those new clothes. They shimmer in the light; they dance with light, and they seem to match your new feelings about your body. As you go down the path of this forest, you are lighter on your feet. You dance or skip. You are filled with the joy of being there, being alive, and being you. You look around and remember you brought another person with you and he has had an experience in the pool, and beneath the waterfall. This person too, looks different, and you give thanks for this and rejoice with him; you rejoice that he is renewed and different and alive.

You continue down the path until you come to a figure that is standing in the path. This is a ancient figure, a sage with long hair, a long robe, and kind face. You sense there is wisdom, and you sense without being told that this is someone who will answer a question for you, something that you have been wanting to know for a long time. He will answer your loved one's questions, too, and you don't even have to speak the question aloud. You just think the question in your mind and your heart, and you listen to the answer in your mind and heart as you stand before the sage.

Pause

Whatever answer you've received is your answer for now, and you look and see that your loved one has received his answer too. You go down the path as it leads out of the forest and into the sunlight, and you joyously soak up the sunlight, the warmth, and the love you feel. Allow yourself to come back to this place but before you do, stop outside, somewhere in the courtyard or wherever you choose.

You sense that you want to give a blessing. Raise your hands, the way a priest does with open palms and upraised hands, and give your blessing of love and light and joy. Give this blessing in one direction and then another, until you have given blessings in every direction,. Know that everyone in this place, everyone in this community, and everyone on this planet has received your blessing. As you stand there, feel the reflection, the reflection of the blessing back to you.

Quietly give thanks. "Father, thank you for this time and for the realization of your love and your light and your life and your joy; we are grateful, and we give thanks. Amen.

Jack Kern, who call himself a "continual seeker" has been the minister of the Unity Church in Naples, Florida, since its inception in 1968. Formerly a businessman, he has been a Unity Minister for 32 years previously serving in Boston and St. Louis.

47

Let Go Fear

Guide: Larry Moen

"The more you open yourself, the more you will find Universal Energy to assist you."

Introduction

We often respond to catching the flu by intensely contracting our bodies to gain strength to fight against the pain. We become physically protective through our muscles to safe-coat ourselves, and we withdraw so that the pain will not affect us. This is in direct contrast to a way in which we could respond, and it is in direct correlation to a way that we protect our Souls from abuse or from getting hurt. Oftentimes, we mentally and even physically condense ourselves into a protective ball to surround and safeguard our Soul.

To experience eternal belief and affection, we must let go of fear and become open to the extraordinary ways of on-going health and well-being. To be able to See without using our eyes. To Feel without touching. To Hear in the silence. To Taste beyond sensation. With eyes closed and an open heart, Feel all the Goodness and Peace that already exists deep within.

Exercise

After you have made all your bedtime preparations, get comfortable in your nice, warm, cozy bed. Dim the lights or turn them off. Lie on your back extending your arms in a "T" position. Agree to be receptive to this experience. Place your palms up (to receive) and slightly separate your legs, keeping them straight, but with soft knees. (Locked knees are bad for your lower back.) You may become so relaxed that you will fall asleep quickly... or you may remain in this position for thirty minutes.

It's best to do this every night, whether you are awake or asleep. You are sending the message to yourself by using your body that you are not fearful and you are receptive to opening to life and letting go. Verbally state "I am not fearful now although I have been fearful of some of the events, people, situations in my life." Reflect on these. Forgive the person or situation. Now, forgive yourself.

The Journey

You are capable of incredible accomplishments! Start by taking a slow deep breath. Open your chest and give your heart room to expand.... Exhale and allow your barrier walls to drop. Now inhale expanding the chest, opening the heart even more.... Exhale and let go.... Let go of your conscious life, of your ego. Inhale again, expanding your chest even wider and still give your heart even more room to expand.

Feel yourself opening to the marvels of life. Until this moment your closed mindedness and fear may have prevented you from seeing things you are here to see. Letting yourself go opens you to one form of seeing the importance of what you are here to do. You are now open to receive the preciousness of everyone and everything. You see more openly now... with more love, acceptance, and compassion.

Pause

Your body is a vehicle—and it matters not what happens to it. Your body is simply a vehicle for your soul. Your true essence is soul and that is really all that matters. The outer covering that you have, that you were born with helps you function through this life only. You are here in this life because you are given an opportunity to work out your own karma. You are given this opportunity to do the best you can during this time on earth, and to be appreciative of this gift of life.

Inhale a slow deep breath, expanding your chest and opening your heart.... Exhale and allow your body to deflate into a mass of physical manifestation.... As you inhale, disconnect yourself from your physical body and merge into your heart. Become the heart of love itself. Become aware of this new sensation with each breath.

Pause

Be without malice and go in peace. You are calmness and peace. Release all judgement, and hold in your heart care and concern for those around you for you are they and they are you. Who knows better than you. To let go is to be open to caring. To be caring is to be loving and to be loving is to become an enlightened being. This is where your truth is. You are on a journey... a journey of transformation. When you let go, you discover everything you need lies within you.

Now let go of this guided imagery and as you drop off to

sleep, sense this freedom will be part of your new life tomorrow morning.

This journey was inspired and nurtured by Andrea White who reads guided imagery over WXCI radio in North Salem, New York.

Larry Moen is the editor and driving force behind the Meditations *series. As a Vietnam veteran, Mr. Moen has been aware that significant emotional events can influence one's life. Mr. Moen discovered that past programming from childhood forward can be healed and transformed using the powers of guided meditation. Subsequently, Mr. Moen embarked on an intensive study of guided visualization which he incorporates in his work with T'ai Chi, yoga and self-hypnosis. He currently leads meditation groups and speaks at seminars.*

48

Sailing Dolphins

Guide: Lisa Zimmer

"Learn to recognize your own blocks and move beyond them."

Introduction

In working with people, I have noticed three general areas that block one's desire or achievement of set goals. In this journey the water represents open-mindedness which can assist you in releasing your own barriers. This visualization can help you in confronting issues and in becoming more receptive to changes. I recommend this imagery in times when you feel blocked in your personal growth or during the decision-making process.

The Journey

Begin by taking a deep breath and releasing tension upon exhalation. Continue breathing deeply throughout this journey to relax yourself completely. Find yourself aboard a well-equipped sailboat with a very capable captain who is instructed to take you sailing for the day.

Find yourself releasing tension as you sail out into the water....

As your sailboat sails effortlessly on the calm ocean, stretch out and feel the warmth of the sun on your body.

Pause

You look alongside the boat to find three dolphins playing. Their graceful bodies glide easily along with the sailboat. As you look closer, you notice words printed upon the animals' backs.

The first one has the word INSECURITIES printed upon him, and as your eyes link together with those of the dolphin, you feel an overwhelming bolt of energy emanate from him to you. You are suddenly empowered with confidence and self-assurance about all of your assets. The word INSECURITIES has now changed to CONFIDENCE. You thank him for his love and insight, and you say good-bye to him as he swims off in the water.

Pause

The second dolphin has the word FEAR printed upon her back, yet when you link eyes with her, a powerful surge of energy is generated from her to you. Your fears now seem humorous as you realize that you have control over your fears and that nothing will prevent your growth. The word FEAR is transformed into the word COURAGE. You thank her for her lesson as you say good-bye and she swims out into the blue water.

Pause

The third dolphin has the word LONELINESS written upon it, and as your eyes link with its eyes, the word LONELINESS has changed to the word FULFILLMENT. You automatically feel a sense of oneness with all life. You connect with it and the birds overhead. The captain now becomes a connector to your appreciation of oneness. From here on, all people will be as one with you. You will now be able to draw what you think you need from yourself in time of despair.

The third dolphin guides your boat to shore, and then bids you farewell as you embrace a new perception of living. When you have accepted this feeling, allow yourself to open your eyes.

Lisa Zimmer is a metaphysical consultant in Naples, Florida. She teaches classes on developing intuition and creative visualization.

Inner Child

49

Baby Pictures

Guide: Edie Weinstein-Moser, M.S.W.

"As adults, we often forget
we were once innocent children."

Introduction

By renewing the relationship with our "childselves" we can discover that even in the midst of chaos, all is well As adults we often forget that an innocent children we needed — and still need — care and protection. This meditation allows the adult to support and nurture that child that he or she once was — and that still exists within.

The Journey

Allow yourself to get comfortable in your favorite chair, perhaps wrapped in a cozy blanket. Feel yourself supported by the soft cushions so that you have no need to hold up any part of your body. This is a time to be nurtured and loved, not a time to struggle even a bit.... That's good. Now... draw in one... long... deep breath that seems to come up from the very depths of your being. And then... release the breath in one... long... sigh. Ahhhhhh.... Let go of anything that may be holding you back... anything that may be preventing you from relaxing. Take another breath, only this time, let it come from a place even deeper than the last one.... Feel your body sinking deeper and deeper into the chair, immersing yourself in its warmth and safety. Know for certain that you are safe and sound and that you will continue to feel secure. All is well.

Pause

As you continue to breathe deeply and fully, your body relaxes more and more.... With each breath, you experience a sense of serenity unlike any you have encountered.... What a nice feeling.

In your mind's eye, allow a picture to appear. At first it may be a bit fuzzy, but tune it in as you would an image on a TV screen. This is a photograph from your past... from your childhood... the earliest recollection you have. See yourself as you were at that age.... How old are you? What do you look like? What are you wearing? Are you alone or is there someone else in the picture? Look at your surroundings, are you somewhere familiar? Remember that as you view this picture, you are completely safe and secure in your chair. Emotions may surface... let them... you are safe. You may feel like laughing or crying... allow yourself the freedom to express whatever arises for you... you are safe.

Pause

Now, stretch your imagination a bit and admit your adult self, as you are now, into the picture. Sit down next to the little you, without touching. Look closely at this tiny creature, so fragile and helpless, counting on other people for safety and nurturing. What feelings awaken within you? Pick this diminutive person up in your arms, cradling him or her tenderly, looking down with eyes of love. The child's eyes meet yours, so full of trust and wonder. This is you, so many years ago. You have been through so much joy and pain, so much success and failure, you have the wisdom of having lived. What do you want to tell this little person?

Pause

Now, gently place the tot back in the picture, planting a kiss on his or her forehead, knowing that you have imparted a sense of certainty that he or she is loved beyond measure.

Now, allow the picture to fade back into memory, knowing that this and so many others are there for you to explore in complete and total safety. As you continue to breathe easily, allow yourself to become more aware of the chair supporting you... of the sound of this voice, of the sensations in your body... move and stretch as you need to... take care of yourself... as you feel your eyes flutter open.... Welcome back.

Edie Weinstein-Moser, M.S.W., is co-publisher of "Visions Magazine" in Miami, Florida. The publication focuses on psychology, health, fitness, the environment, as well as peace, and social justice issues. She also works with individuals and groups in facilitating personal growth.

50

Happy Inner Child

Guide: Geneva B. Mitchell, D.C.H.

"Beautiful possibilities are available by contacting the 'child' and communicating with the hurt part."

Introduction

Reading this script into a tape recorder and listening to it daily, can change your life. So many people have hidden emotional problems, and this meditation helps to expand learning and belief in self. It also provides knowledge for greater self control.

The Journey

Close your eyes, breathe deeply, and think of some areas of your life that are not going the way you wish. Choose one specific thing that you would like to change or accomplish. See it clearly. Don't worry about how you get to this position, just see yourself at that place now.

Begin drifting away and stop the thinking. If a thought comes into your mind, let it go out, like the wind coming in and out an open window. Hear the count, and count along — 20, 19, 18, deep, deep relaxation — 17, 16, 15, 14, down, down—heavy relaxed feelings in your toes, knees and thighs

— 13, 12, 11, 10, 9, 8, so calm, so peaceful, so serene, 7, 6, 5, 4, 3, 2, 1, 0 — all parts of you are heavy and relaxed. Your body is so relaxed, so relaxed. All body functions are in harmony, and in this relaxed state, they function in total perfection.

Now your mind is relaxed. In this relaxed state, the mind is open and receptive, ready and able. It is willing to accept positive input as you unlearn all your learned limitations. Discover your own inner abilities and potentials and your willingness to rely upon your own subconscious mind to help you do anything that is of value or interest to you. In the past, your subconscious has had little opportunity to give recognition to its own ways of understanding. It now has that opportunity. The subconscious mind has a tremendous capacity for learning. We all have so many abilities — abilities we can't even imagine. Abilities that can now be discovered by you in your own way, in your own time. Time can be condensed, and time can be expanded.

So in this deep, deep, state everything is possible. As you visualize and imagine yourself as you desire to be, you become as you want to be. Take as long as you wish. Be wherever you want to be, for as long as you want. As you visualize a scene, for instance if you are above a rocky mountain, look down and see large, huge boulders on this mountain. Look closer, and you see cactuses in bloom. You see brilliant reds and yellows spreading like a carpet of reds and yellows, with green interspersed across an expanse as far as the eye can see. From your vantage point, you are unable to see the stickers and thorns, unable to see beneath the beauty of the blooming flowers. Life is like this. To see clearer and clearer, you need to get closer. You get closer and closer and see cactuses are beautiful. The spikes are tortuous. You turn over and view the clear, blue sky. As you drift away from this mountain, you notice a beautiful oasis with trees, water, and grass. You drift down to be beneath a lovely, large willow tree. A spring is swiftly moving along, and you walk near the bank to watch the rushing water. You see shining rocks and colors sparkling as the sun plays through the leaves of the tree.

Remove your shoes and put your feet on the sandy shore. Wiggle your toes in the sand, and notice how good the warm sand feels. Now you decide to test the water with one of your toes. It's so cold you can only keep your toe in for a moment. You prefer the warm sand. Return your toe to the sand and begin to wiggle both your feet deep into it. Feel the warmth of the sand as you wiggle deeper. The sand covers your feet, your legs, your abdomen, your spine, neck, arms and hands. It's wonderful. Stay a while and enjoy the warmth.

Pause

Now ease out of your sand cocoon and begin to play as a child plays. Have fun, —skip, hop, laugh, set your inner child free. Swing your arms and legs. Find respect within yourself for your child and then quietly settle down while your child rests. Hug your child. Let your child know the adult part of you better. Let the child know you respect the child. Agree with your child that there are times when it's appropriate to feel angry or hurt, and you respect that. Now share with your child that you've been hurt and allow the child to share with you his or her hurts Let the child's anger and hurt surface and acknowledge the feelings; give them credence, and let them go. The hurt part is released; it floats to the surface and rushes off into the fast flowing stream.

Each time you release these angers, hurts, and fearful feelings, you feel lighter and lighter. Hug your child and continue hugging your child, so your child knows you love and understand his feelings. Use your adult knowledge and sincerity to allow your child freedom to respond in a child's manner. See yourself and your child now smiling and having mutual feelings of respect and love. Do whatever you feel like doing with your child now and feel good. Rest for awhile. Know inner peace, forgive past hurts and continue on into the future feeling integrated, whole, and happy... very happy.

Geneva B. Mitchell is founder and director of New Image Hypnosis Center in Albuquerque, New Mexico. She is a dedicated, motivated hypnotherapist with many interests such as writing and public speaking. She has recently published two books entitled "Take The Power" and "This Life is Yours."

51

New Moon

Guide: Chrystle Clae

"Connect with the inner child and feel joy of life."

Introduction

This imagery aids the inner "you" in learning to be less judgmental of yourself and of others. Getting in touch with the inner child is one way to feel the joy of life.

The Journey

Imagine through your mind's eye that you are in a cool and fragrant Oriental garden. There's a pond filled with rainbow-colored fish in this garden. The air is clear with a gentle breeze. You're approaching a big old tree with low friendly branches. It is nighttime, and the garden is lit by a full moon and soft Japanese lanterns hanging from the trees. Hanging from the big sturdy tree, there is a secure swing with a cushion for you to sit on. As you sit down... lean back and look up to the sky filled with bright and lively stars that seem to be blinking to assure you and the universe of their life.

As you feel the wind on your face and arms, relax and enjoy the movement of the swing up and down. Imagine for a moment that you are a child again... in a child's strong and supple body... your spirit brimming with joy and peace. You're a child swinging on this warm, fragrant night. The jasmine blossoms, lilacs, and roses fill the air with their light perfumes. How does it feel to be child in this protected environment? If you could, what would you most like to do... as a child. Go ahead and do it. See yourself. Think of a way you could do this at your current age. Slowly and gradually come to a stop as you resume your current age.

As your feet touch the ground to support you, you notice a small, white bridge over the pond that leads to another part of the garden. The bridge is also lit by Japanese lanterns, hanging from the trees that border it. As you begin to cross the bridge and come to the center of it, look into the water at the lanterns reflection, see the different colors stream into each other... look closer now and see your own reflection... see yourself as you look when you feel "whole"... "complete"... "full." If you have difficulty seeing yourself this way... remember a time when you did something that made you really feel satisfied. It may have been a completion of a job or a good deed you did. How you felt when you heard an uplifting speech or song, a time when you were genuinely happy for someone else... a time when you felt loved, without condition — a time of inspiration.... Look into the water and see yourself in this "complete" state. You might recognize that this was a time when you felt your connection to God. You allowed that energy to become the greatest part of you... if only for a moment. Feel yourself as Light, brimming with love to give, brimming with the love you've received... knowing all the questions and knowing all the answers. Take a moment and feel your oneness with all there is... as you take a deep, refreshing breath of this perfect night air.

Continue to walk across the bridge, and as you reach the other side of this rippling pond you see a gazebo. The lanterns in the gazebo give off a soft, lavender-blue light as they hang from each pillar. Go inside and sit down in the big, rounded chair, with the soft seat and back cushions. Sit there and relax as you sense a newness to your body... a freshness to your mind... a brightness to your spirit.

In this quiet, comfortable place, let's imagine many things—a world where we can see the light within each other—in our quest for oneness with all life. Imagine that you become each of the following... one at a time... without judgment, pity, or gratification. Become one with a... plant... bird... sea creature... an animal... an insect... child... disabled person ... elderly person... someone who is beautiful to look at.

Realize as you breathe deeply that you are one with all life and feel your connection to the Divine as you carry it with you in the week ahead.

Chrystle Clae is an astrologer, psychic counselor, and teacher in Seminole, Florida. She is a nationally-known writer on the subject of metaphysics and she has a column for psychic advice in the "Suncoast Beach Reporter." She is listed in "Who's Who in Service to the Earth."

52

Play

Guide: Margot Escott, M.S.W.

"When adults allow themselves to engage in spontaneous, non-competitive play, the magical, playful inner child is able to emerge."

Introduction

I have been helping people access their inner child through play for many years. The focus in inner child work is to get in touch with all aspects of ourselves. In working with adults on healing and loving their inner child, I have found that we need to make contact with our playful child. This journey is helpful for any adult, especially those who feel responsible for everyone else's happiness and neglect their own. By getting into positive childhood play experiences, we can reconnect with our creative, energetic selves. After this meditation, you may find you are able to go back to a difficult problem or challenge with a different perspective and greater ability to see solutions. I hope using this imagery will inspire readers to find ways to develop play in their adult lives.

The Journey

Allow yourself to relax — focus on your breath — breathing in and breathing out. Take some deep breaths from your abdomen and with each exhale, let yourself relax even deeper. Allow your breath to become regular and even. If you have any thoughts, imagine a fluffy white cloud gently pushing those thoughts from your conscious mind and allow your unconscious mind to take over. Bring your attention to your breath, with each exhale entering a more profound state of deep peace.

As you drift deeper into a pleasant state of relaxation, imagine yourself standing in a beautiful spot of nature. It is a warm, sunny day, and there is a gentle breeze caressing your face. In the background, you hear the song of birds and start to become aware of the laughter of small children. You see that you are in a wonderful playground, with every imaginable type of playground equipment. There are slides, swings, seesaws, jungle gyms, and many other things. These things are made out of whatever material you want them to be, any size and color that feels right for you. You watch the children playing with abandon and joy. Some of them beckon to you to join them, and as you approach them, you become smaller and smaller until you reach a size and age that feels comfortable for you. You feel all kinds of joyful, exciting feelings as you begin to explore all the activities that are available to you. You are fearless and adventuresome as you climb and swing and play. Let yourself remain in this playful state for the next few minutes. Be aware of what it feels like to touch, to bounce, to slide and to fly through the air. Begin to be aware of the smells that surround you — the wood, metal, sand, and the other children. What other smells can you recall at the playground? Allow yourself to be totally immersed in this scene, using all of your senses.

Feel free to create other types of games, with or without the other children. You may to invite a favorite pet to play with you. Remember, this is your vision to create as you wish.

When you are ready, say good-bye to the playground and your friends. As you start to walk away, you become larger and larger until you reach your normal size. Know that you can return to your playground whenever you wish.

Margot Escott, M.S.W. is a social worker in private practice in Naples, Florida where she works with chemically addicted individuals. She has developed and conducted workshops on "The Healing Power of Humor," "Discovering the Inner Child through Play" and "Visualization for Success" throughout the country. She also helped to develop a Humor Wagon at Naples Community Hospital.

Receiving Gifts & Love

53

Gifts of the Garden

Guide: Karen Carnabucci

"Learning experiences can be enhanced through symbolic review using imagery."

Introduction

At the conclusion of a learning experience, especially seminars and workshops, it is helpful to review and integrate symbolically what has been studied and observed. This imagery offers a closure through the use of archetypes and symbols that helps the listener process the previous activities.

The Journey

Give yourself permission to relax your body in a comfortable space and in a comfortable position as we begin to breathe deeply and slowly. Take a deep breath into your lungs, holding for a moment and then breathing out, allowing yourself to sigh as you exhale.... Another deep breath in, and then breathing out with a sigh, and a third breath in, and out again with a sigh.... Allow the floor, chair, or pillows to fully support your body so that your only task now is to continue to breathe, maintaining an alertness as you continue to relax.... When you are ready to begin, become aware of a container at your feet.... Take this container, knowing it is time to leave this room or space and begin your journey. You discover yourself walking outside on a warm and sunny day and turning left to find a grassy path. In the distance, you see a wall and you decide to walk closer to investigate it.... As you approach, the form of the wall becomes clearer to you, and you see a gate that is part of this wall. As you stand at the gate, take note of the quality of the wall, the form and material of the gate, and how it feels to be standing here.

Pause

Now you notice a key to the gate, perhaps hanging on a hook nearby, perhaps on the ground, perhaps somewhere else. Take the key now, and fit it into the lock, turning it. The gate swings open, and you step through the doorway.

Moving to the other side, you discover yourself in an exquisite garden, the landscape lushly planted with flowers, vines, shrubs, and trees of every description.... Take time now to look at the plantings in this garden. As you do, you realize that each of the four seasons are represented: the delicate flowering bulbs and dogwood saplings of spring, the fragrant roses and peonies of summer, the bright chrysanthemums and ripening fruits of autumn, and the stately evergreens and red holly berries of winter. You explore each planting now, noting the special beauty of each.

As you move across the garden, your attention is caught by the sound of children's laughter. You see a pathway of colored stones, and you decide to follow the sound as you take this path. You find a juggler, gaily throwing colored balls into the air and catching them with ease. The juggler sees you and smiles, catching the balls neatly in one hand. Then he puts his other hand into his pocket and pulls out a gift that is meant for you. You take this gift, thank him, and put it into the container that you are carrying.

The path leads you now to a lake, and you are again alone. As you bend down or kneel down at the water's edge, you intuitively know that there is a gift meant especially for you in this lake. Put your hand into the water, feeling its refreshing coolness, take what is meant for you, and put it into your container.... The path winds back to the plantings of the seasons, and again you know that you may take what is meant for you. Notice all that is there in the flower and herb beds, the fruit orchard, and the vegetable garden and take what you need for today, adding to your container.

Pause

Then you know it is time to leave this garden. You again find yourself at the gate and once again step through the opening, pulling the gate closed behind you. Secure the gate with the key and begin your return.

Become aware of the position of your body, your breathing, and the sound of this voice. When you are ready, allow yourself to open your eyes and be present in this room.

Karen Carnabucci is a therapist specializing in experiential therapies, including psychodrama, family sculpture, and imagery, in her work with adult children of alcoholics and dysfunctional families. A former newspaper writer and editor, she is a consulting therapist at Caron Family Services, affiliated with the Caron Foundation and internationally recognized drug and alcohol treatment center in Wernersville, Pa. She recently collaborated on a book, "Intimacy: The Quest for Connection."

54

Loving Kindness

Guide: Stephen Levine

"This meditation uses the conceptual word-oriented mindscape in perhaps its most skillful manner. It turns a hindrance into an ally."

Introduction

"Loving Kindness" meditation works with a different level of thought — of name and form, of duality, of "I" and "other" — as a means of healing long-conditioned separation into the unconditional oneness of being. "Loving Kindness" meditation concentrates healing on a level of mind that usually numbs the heart. Indeed our work is not so much to open the heart — which like the sun is always shining, but whose light is often obscured — but to open the mind so that the deep light of the essence of mind we call the heart can shine through.

By cultivating loving kindness in that aspect of mind that usually lives life as an afterthought, we change the context of our existence. We begin to live directly. We awaken.

The Journey

Sitting comfortably, allow the attention to come gradually to the breath... The breath coming and going all by itself deep within the body... take a few moments to allow the attention to gather within the even rhythm of the breath... turning gently within, begin to direct, toward yourself, care for your own well-being. Begin to look on yourself as though you were your only child. Have mercy on you. Silently in the heart say, "May I be free from suffering. May I be at peace." Just feel the breath breathing into the heart space as we relate to ourselves with kindness and care... Allow the heart, silently, to whisper the words of mercy that heal, that open. "May I be free from suffering. May I be at peace." Allow yourself to be healed.... Whispering to yourself, send wishes for your own well-being: "May I be free from suffering. May I be at peace." Repeat gently with each in-breath into the heart, "May I be free from suffering." With each out-breath, "May I be at peace...." With the next in-breath, "May I be free from suffering." With the following out-breath, "May I be at peace." Repeat these words slowly and gently with each in-breath, with each out-breath... Not as a prayer but as an extension of loving care to yourself.

Notice what limits this love, this mercy, this willingness to be whole, to be healed. "May I be free from suffering. May I be at peace." Continue with this rhythm, this deepening of merciful joy and loving kindness drawn in with each breath, expanding with each exhalation. "May I be free from suffering. May I be at peace." Let the breath continue naturally, as mercy for yourself, your only child, for this being within.

Though at first these may only feel like words echoing from the mind, gently continue. There can be no force here. Force closes the heart. Let the heart receive the mind in a new tenderness and mercy. "May I be free from suffering. May I be at peace." Each breath deepening the nurturing warmth of relating to oneself with loving kindness and compassion.

Each exhalation deepening in peace, expanding into the spaciousness of being, developing the deep patience that does not wait for things to be otherwise, but relates with loving kindness to things as they are. "May I be free from suffering. May I be at peace."

Allow the healing in with each breath. Allow your true spacious nature. Continue for a few breaths more this drawing in, this opening to, loving kindness. Relating to yourself with great tenderness, sending well-being into your mind and body, embrace yourself with these gentle words of healing. Now gently bring to mind someone for whom you have a feeling of warmth and kindness. Perhaps a loved one or teacher or friend. Picture this loved one in your heart. With each in-breath whisper to him or her, "May you be free from suffering. May you be at peace." With each breath draw that loved one into your heart, "May you be free from suffering." With each out-breath filling them with your loving kindness, "May you be at peace." With the next inhalation drawing their heart closer to yours, "May you be free from suffering." With the following out-breath extending to the loved one a wish for his well-being, "May you be at peace."

Continue to breathe the loved one into your heart, whispering silently to yourself, to him, "May you be free from suffering. May you be at peace." Continue the gentle breath of connection, the gentle wish for their happiness and wholeness. Let the breath be breathed naturally, softly, lovingly into the heart, coordinated with your words, with your concentrated feelings of loving kindness and care. "May you be free of suffering. May you know the deepest levels of peace." Send them your love, your compassion, your care. Breathing them in and through your heart. "May you be free from suffering. May you know your deepest joy, your greatest peace." And as you sense them in your heart, sense this whole world that wishes so to be healed, to know its true nature, to be at peace. Now to yourself say, "Just as I wish to be happy so do all sentient beings." And in your heart with each in-breath, with each out-breath, whisper, "May all beings be free of suffering. May all beings be at peace." Let your loving kindness reach out to all beings as it did to your loved one, sensing all beings in need of healing, in need of the peace of their true nature. "May all beings be at peace. May they be free of suffering." "May all sentient beings, to the most recently born, be free of fear, free of pain. May all beings heal into their true nature. May all beings know the absolute joy of absolute being." "May all beings everywhere be at peace. May all beings be free of suffering." The whole planet like a bubble floating in the ocean of your heart.

Each breath draws in the love that heals the world, that deepens the peace we all seek. Each breath feeds the world with the mercy and compassion, the warmth and patience that quiets the mind and opens the heart. "May all beings be free from suffering. May all beings be at peace." Let the breath come softly. Let the breath go gently. Wishes of well-being and mercy, of care, of loving kindness, are extended to this world we all share. "May all beings be free of suffering. May all beings dwell in the heart of healing. May all beings be at peace."

55

Songs of the Sea

Guide: Annette Covatta

"Unwind and relax in the presence of the sea."

Introduction

Relating the sounds of the sea to songs can create an intimate inner link between the unsolved mysteries of your life and the flowing within of love. This visualization works by letting the dynamism of the sea lead you through your inner process. The results of this imagery have been — to borrow from Anne M. Lindburgh — "Gifts of the Sea." This imagery is particularly helpful when you feel stuck or blocked in your life. Read it slowly and in small bites.

The Journey

Take some moments to drift inside your body. Focus on your circulatory system — the life-energy flowing through your body and into the extremities of toes, genitals, finger-tips, and crown of your head. Feel your body alive and awake to the circulating movement of the fluids in your arteries, veins, and pores. Be fully present in the flow of this life-energy. Allow the movement of your breath to weave with the life-energy — the Qi, as the Chinese name it. Let your conscious thoughts drop away so that you can experience an emptiness, a lightness of the mind. Rest in this open space for as long as you need to feel connected to your inner quiet.

Pause

Now to go to the sea or the ocean. Choose a body of water that is familiar to you or attracts you in some way. See it as if through a telescopic lens — the panoramic view. Use all your senses to be fully there: What are the sounds... the tastes... colors... smells? Then, choose a spot where you can feel a deep connection with the sea: a particular boulder or rock... the edge of a cliff... the end of a dock... a hidden cove... a sandy beach plot. Sit or lie down there. Let your eyes drink in the scene, and listen... listen... listen....

The sea contains many voices that sing her mysteries. There are lilting rhythms and powerful energies in her songs. The songs of the sea well up from the consciousness of our planet. They express the multi-glories of creation. They express the glory of humanity. Songs of peace, excitement, agony, abundance, suffering, passion, and high play. The ebb and flow of the waves are like the tension and release of human living.

Take time to connect to the feelings stirring inside you now. What songs does the sea sing in your heart? Let the sounds of the sea bring to life the deep resonances of your present life — the life you are living now. Is this a time of serenity and peace? suffering? challenge? expansion?... What do you seek from these waters? healing? cleansing? clarity? groundedness? patience? integration? peace?... Take all the time you need to let the waves and flowing waters wash over you, knowing that the gifts you seek are already present in your heart.

Pause

Feel the wonders and mysteries of the ocean. Feel the wonders and mysteries of the heart. Feel the wonders and mysteries of *your* heart. They are born of the same energy.

And now, look around you. You will notice many shells and stones of all sizes, shapes, and colors. Roam about in your space and choose a shell or stone that seems to be in harmony with what your heart is seeking at this time of your life. You will feel yourself being drawn to some concrete object near you. Pick it up and explore it in your hand—its texture, size, color, shape. As you open your senses to the object, be attentive to the message it holds for you. Take all the time you need for this.

Now, walk to the waterfront. You may throw the object into the sea as a prayer-offering and gesture of oneness with the universe or you may want to keep your sea-object with you.

Linger awhile there, feeling the wind, smelling the air, listening to the waves and looking at the water, sky, and earth.

When you feel ready, leave the seashore and walk back slowly, returning to the room. Gently let your eyes open.

Annette Covatta, D.M.A., has a lifetime involvement in the arts and personal growth programs, and she holds a Doctor of Musical Arts from Boston University. Ms. Covatta is the founder and director of FULCRUM, whose mission is to enable persons to reach their potential through the body/mind/spirit/soul connection. Through FULCRUM, she presents workshops which reflect her interest in the creative process and wholistic spirituality.

Grief

56

Grief

Guide: Stephen Levine

"One need not have experienced the death of a loved one in order to find this exploration useful. It makes room in our heart for our pain, for our healing, for our life."

Introduction

Along the path of healing that leads into the heart, one is called upon to examine grief. Grief is the binding alloy of the armoring around the heart. As if touched by fire, the mind recoils at losing what it holds most dear. As the mind contracts around its grief, the spaciousness of the heart often seems very distant.

Some believe they have no grief. This is another aspect of our rigid denial and self-protection. Some may say, "I haven't lost anyone—why should I be grieving?" If only it were that simple.

Most think of grief as a momentous sadness, but it is much subtler than that. Everyone has grief. Everyone seems to have some unbalanced tally sheet with life, some unfinished business. An incompleteness with the past and with ourselves, a fatiguing self-consciousness, the predominant theme of the unfinished symphony of mind's yearning.

Our grief manifests as a self-judgment, as fear, as guilt, as anger and blame. It is the insistent mercilessness with ourselves and a world that we hardly let within. Our grief is our fear of loss, our fear of the unknown, our fear of death. Our fear of what is coming around the next unknown corner. Grief is the rope burns left behind when what we have held on to most dearly is pulled out of reach, beyond our grasp.

At subtler levels one sees that the tendency of the mind to hold, to cling and condemn, to judge, is a daily aspect of our grief. A feeling of "not-enoughness" that longs to become otherwise.

The Journey

Find a comfortable place to sit in a quiet room... Take a few moments to settle into the quietness... Gradually bring your attention to the center of the chest... Let awareness gather at that place of high sensitivity... Notice any ache at the center... Is there a physically painful quality to your mental longing?

With the thumb, press gently into this point of grief and love... Begin gradually to exert pressure on that point... Feel the sternum, the bone beneath, as though it were the armoring over the opening to the heart. As though it were that which so often blocks entrance to your spacious nature. Slowly, without force, but with mercy and steadiness, push into that point... Press in gently but firmly. Let the pain into your heart. Breathe that pain through that point into your heart.

Stop pushing it away... Push into it instead... Let it in... Breathe that pain in through the griefpoint... Let your thumb push steadily, but without force, into that ache, and let awareness enter that point of sensation at the center of the chest. A merciful awareness, using the pressure on the griefpoint to enter through years of accumulated sediment of unfelt, unexpressed, unexamined feelings. Penetrating the exhaustion of our everyday, ordinary grief compressed hard as rock.

Push into the pain. Past the resistance to life. Past the fear, the self-doubt, the distrust. Past feelings of being unsafe. Past all that holding around being unloved. Past the ten thousand moments of putting yourself out of your heart. The judgment, the longing, the anger. Past years of hidden grief. The shame and secret fears, and unrequited loves you have spoken of to no one.

Let the pain in at last. Have mercy on yourself. Let it in. Let life in at last. Breathe that pain into your heart. Past the holdings and armoring of a lifetime. Let it in. Let it in at last.

Let your heart break. All the losses, all the injuries, all the grief, of a lifetime dumped there, layer after layer holding you back from your life. Holding you out of your heart. Push in... Breathe that into your heart. Let your heart at last experience all those parts of your life you have pushed away. So little room in our hearts for our pain. Let it in. Receive it with mercy instead of fear or judgement. Cradle your pain in your heart. Let each breath gently rock that cradle.

Now draw in with each breath, all the pain in your heart you have tried so long not to feel. All the headlines we try to push away. All the news of a suffering world. The whole world on fire within and without. So much grasping to the burning embers of our longing and our dread. All those children starving with bulging bellies and watery eyes. The ten thousand flies that come to eat them. All the women, all the men, who have abused and are being abused at this very moment. All the suffering of the world unfolding in this very instant. All of their pain. All of your pain.

Breathe it in... Let it in. And your children will die. And your grandchildren... Breathe it in. Fear says stop, but gently continue in mercy for yourself and the deep healing. Push in gently to the fear... Gently but firmly. Not as punishment but as a willingness to go beyond old protections and devices for escape. Past the old fears. Have mercy on you. Let this pain you have been trying to elude come into the heart of healing. So much pain. So much posturing. So much hiding there. A lifetime of fear, of anger, of distrust. Let it in... Let it in. It is so hard to live armored and frightened, unavailable to life, to ourselves. Have mercy. Let the tender heart receive all those parts of you that say it is self-indulgent to forgive yourself. That cruel, merciless judgmental mind. that cold indifference toward the suffering of others and ourselves. Let these griefs dissolve into the opening heart.

Breathe them into your heart. Let them melt. Let them be healed. Let us get on with our lives. All the pain in this world, all the fear of this world. All the moments we have hated ourselves. All the moments we would have rather been dead, armored right there at the center of the chest, melting. All the times we couldn't say what we wanted to because we were afraid we wouldn't be loved. All the times we wondered what love really was. All the times we were disappointed, there at the center of the chest. So much holding. Breathe that pain into your heart... Let it in... Let it in. Each breath drawn in through the griefpoint carries the pain right into the center of our heart.

So much room in our heart for our pain when we let go of the armoring and resistance. It is difficult to open to this grief-pain in our tiny body, in our fragile mind, so breathe it into the enormous heart. This heart of mercy drinks from our pain. Let it in. All the fear that we are less than good in God's eyes, that we are not the beloved... Breathe it in. All the fears that we have fallen out of grace, that we are cursed and unlovable held right there in the griefpoint... Breathe it in... Breathe it in.

A lifetime of pain... Breathe it in. Push into that point.

Notice how part of your grief comes from trying to keep grief under control. This mercilessness with which we reject ourselves repeatedly. This often unkind mind, this fearful child we carry. Have mercy on you. Let it into your heart. Let it break your heart at last... Let it in. Our parents die. Our lovers die. Our children die.

All that we know is in constant change. Constantly being born and proceeding toward death. The people we love most will at times suffer. There is nothing we can do to keep them from their pain. This world is so hard at times... Breathe it in... Let it in. And sometimes our loved ones kill themselves. They can't stand the pain, they can't get through the armoring to the healing just beneath. But you can get through it... Push into that point. That griefpoint in the heart center... Let it in. How long can you elude your life?

So much of ourselves pushed aside. So much shame and mercilessness. All the places we will not forgive ourselves. All the places we are diminished. The despair, the helplessness, breathe it in... Breathe it in... Let the breath take the pain to the center of your heart. The heart has room for it all... Let it in. Have mercy on you. Let the pain in past the fear.

All the moments that we weren't loved and weren't loving. All the parts of ourselves we've coldly disregarded, regard now with mercy at the griefpoint and warmly draw them into the healing heart. All the self-cruelty. All our unwillingness to love ourselves. All our judgment. Each breath bringing old mind into the heart, melting in the embrace of such kindness and care. Fear melting. Doubt melting. The armoring falling away, exposing the luminescent whorl of the heart center. Our shimmering nature discovered just beyond our pain. The sense of loss flickering in the enormity.

Each breath drawing in gratitude for the moments shared with those we have loved and lost. And gratitude for the mystery of connection. The fear of a lifetime melting into the heart... Push ever so gently into it... Breathe that healing mercy right into your heart. An enormous energy... Let it in... Just let that energy into your heart... Draw the shadows into the light. The armor is disintegrating. The griefpoint is dissolving into the touchpoint of the heart. Hard-edge sensations softening. Dissolving into loving kindness. Bringing home the lost child. The heart embracing the mind with the soft breath of mercy and the tender caress of forgiveness. As the griefpoint becomes the heartpoint, the body begins to hum. Feel the cells like a dry sponge absorbing this mercy and deep kindness.

As the griefpoint surrenders its pain to the heart the pained contents of the mind float in the spaciousness of mercy and awareness. The feelings of separation increasingly becoming a sense of inseparability from that loved one, from ourselves. Now let your hand come gently away from the griefpoint, let your hand settle into your lap... Take the pressure off that point. And notice that there seems to be an opening where the ache used to be... You can feel the touchpoint of the heart when you take your hand away... Breathe in and out of that point. This is the breath of the heart. Let awareness of the flow between the world and your heart be your constant companion. Let the pain which drew your attention to the heart be an initiation into the healing for which you took birth.

May all beings be free of suffering. May all beings focus the spacious heart on the pained mind. May all beings know the joy of their great deathless nature.

In the mid-1970's, while working with Ram Dass ("Grist for the Mill," 1976) Stephen Levine taught meditation in the California prison system. For the next few years he led workshops and learned from the terminally ill the need for deeper levels of healing and the profound joy of service ("A Gradual Awakening," 1979). In 1979 he began teaching workshops with his wife, Ondrea. As co-directors of the Hanuman Foundation Dying Project, as they continued to serve the terminally ill and those deeply affected by loss. Their guided Meditations for Healing grief, heavy emotional states, sexual abuse, and subtler forms of life/death preparation brought them international recognition ("Healing into Life and Death," 1987).

Past Lives

57

Contentment

Guide: Richard J. Palmer

"I use this journey for regressing my clients in order to retrieve from their past something that they have lost or cannot remember."

Introduction

You should be seated and comfortable. Clients have had a pre-introduction interview and are ready to be hypnotized. You should have your legs uncrossed, feet flat on the floor, hands separated. Direct your attention to a spot on the ceiling or an object held in your hand, above your line of vision.

Focus your attention on a spot on the ceiling or on the wall. Let all the tensions of your days activities flow from your mind and body — nothing on your mind. Now you'll find that as you stare at that spot, your eyes want to close or go out of focus. Now take a full deep breath, exhale, and relax. And now a third deep breath and exhale, and feel yourself relaxing and letting go. Count from five down to one as your eyes grow heavy and drowsy and closed by the count of one.

5: Your eyelids are relaxing, growing limp, loose, and heavy.
4: Those heavy eyelids are wanting to close down now,

relaxing and growing heavier and heavier, relaxing, limp and heavy.

3: Each blink is a sign that your eyelids are ready to close down now. Growing heavy, limp and loose.

2: Heavy, closing, closing, closing...

1: Eyelids closed, sleep, deeply! Relax and go deeper now.

*With the command "sleep deeply", snap your fingers loudly — this is the "shock conversion" and deepens the trance. As an alternative, a strong touch on the forehead or shoulder serves the same purpose. A deepening technique should follow immediately.

The Journey

Now that you are in this peaceful state of relaxation, you're going to a wonderful place called "contentment". During this trip, you will be safe and sound. You are going one step beyond the physical boundaries in which we now live. You are going to a place of healing, a place of understanding, a place of relaxation, a place of wisdom, this place called "contentment." To reach this place you must first enter a building called the Limelight Portal. This building is unique because it has five floors up and five floors down. So as you enter the lobby of this building, you notice that the walls are translucent and emit a warm, glowing light. There are masses of beautiful flowers and shrubbery placed appropriately around the lobby. You instantly feel very comfortable and relaxed. You see at the other end of the lobby the words "stairs down." You walk over and start down the stairs, going deeper and deeper. As you progress downward, your relaxation becomes greater and greater. You find yourself looking forward to this journey.

You arrive at the landing of the fourth floor. There is no one here, and it is very quiet and peaceful. You feel as if a heavy weight has been lifted from your shoulders as you drift and float into a deeper and deeper level of total relaxation. You walk to the end of the landing and start down the stairs once again. Down, down, down you go, ever deeper into tranquility. You are feeling very peaceful now as your reach the third floor. The lights on the landing cast a soft, warm glow, and you feel very good about yourself as you continue your downward journey. You go down the stairs to the next floor. Deeper and deeper you go. There is a soothing warmth in the air, and you feel more and more relaxed. You now reach the second floor, and now you are feeling very relaxed and content. You feel so good about yourself and are looking forward to your journey's end. Only one more floor to go. It feels almost as if you are now floating to the end of the landing, where you start down the stairs to the last floor. You go farther and farther down, until you finally arrive at the first floor. You see a sign on the wall and it says, "entrance way to contentment." You enter and find yourself in a room engulfed in a soft, subdued, bluish light. Standing in the room, you can hear the soft strains of some mysterious tune wafting to your ears. There is a cot in the middle of the room. You walk over and lie down and find yourself going into a deeper and deeper relaxed state. As you drift and float into a deeper and deeper state of relaxation, a voice speaks to you.

You have now entered the world of the subconscious. These steps downward into the contentment room have taken you deep into your subconscious where all of your thoughts are stored. Here you will find everything you have ever experienced. All you memories from the fetus stage right up to this present moment.

This contentment room is a long room with shelves all around. Your thoughts are on these shelves. Your most recent thoughts are near the entrance and easy to find. The farther back we go in time, the farther back we go in the recesses of your mind, the farther back in the room you must look. Be diligent and take your time, you will find what you are looking for. We will now start with this question:

(Ask appropriate questions. When you've completed your questioning, use the following trance termination.)

You will now leave this room and upon reaching the fifth floor, you will return to full awareness once again. Now go my friend, you are now a (non-smoker) (person who has learned to eat properly), or whatever other problem you have solved. You arise from your cot and leave the contentment room. You now start up the first flight of stairs, slowly, gently, starting to return to full awareness and feeling wonderfully good about yourself. You reach the second flight of stairs and your pace quickens, as you feel perfect in every way, physically, mentally and emotionally calm, serene and confident. You reach the third flight of steps and you feel a stirring surge of energy. You're becoming more aware of your physical body, and all of your senses are alive and responsive. As you hurry up the fourth flight of stairs, your eyes are beginning to open and your entire body feels refreshed and relaxed, and you feel wonderfully good. You now start up the fifth and last flight of stairs, becoming fully aware, eyes open and sparkling clear. How do you feel?

Richard J. Palmer is a hypnotherapist from Fayetteville, Arkansas, who has practiced clinical hypnotherapy for five years. He specializes in smoking cessation, weight loss, and regression programs.

58

Past Life Regression

Guide: Arthur Cataldo

"Most people find regression helpful in understanding a particular relationship, behavioral pattern, or physical condition."

Introduction

This is the skeleton form of the regression. What happens after the regressee has landed in another time is guided by that individual's needs. It is most important to be flexible. Most people find regression helpful in understanding a particular relationship, behavioral pattern, or physical condition. Once the origin of the condition, pattern, or difficult relationship is understood, the regressee can change his/her emotional reaction (the karmic baggage we carry with us into future lives) through forgiveness of self and the others involved. The emotional nature of the material elicited can be quite strong.

If you are not comfortable with guiding someone through powerful emotions, this process is perhaps best left to those regressionists who also possess counseling and psychotherapeutic skills. Clairvoyant skills also can help regressees to move beyond impasses.

The Journey

Sit or lie down. Make yourself comfortable; remove your shoes; uncross your legs. Close your eyes. Take a deep breath....

Exhale. Take another deep breath; breathe in Peace, Light, and Love... and exhale any mental tension. Release any tension from your neck, head and shoulders.... Take another deep breath, breathing in Peace, Light and Love...

and exhale any emotional tension. Focus on your heart and your solar plexus and feel a centering and a balancing in those places....

Take another deep breath, breathing in Peace, Light, and Love...

and exhale physical tension from anywhere in your body. Let it pour out of your hands, feet, and out the top of your head....

Pause

Let your breathing find its own natural rhythm while you say, "Beloved Mother/Father God, I ask to be filled, surrounded, and protected with the Light of the Holy Spirit. I ask to live beyond earth into areas of Absolute Truth. I ask that which is most needed by this soul in this time will be brought forth. I ask to join together as channels of Light, of Love, of Truth, of Healing, and of Blessing. I stand believing. Thank you Mother/Father."

And with your next breath, imagine a ray of white light entering the soles of your feet, relaxing your feet....

And see and feel the relaxing energy moving up to your ankles, feeling your ankles becoming more and more relaxed....

Now see and feel the relaxing energy moving up to your calves, feeling your lower legs becoming deeply, comfortably relaxed....

Now see and feel the relaxing energy moving up to your knees and upper legs, perhaps beginning to feel pleasant sensations of heaviness and warmth as your leg muscles become more and more relaxed....

Now see and feel the relaxing energy moving up to your hips, buttocks, and genitals, feeling those muscles relaxing completely....

And see and feel the relaxing energy moving up to your lower back and abdomen. Notice how your breathing deepens as your abdominal muscles relax — relaxing deeper and deeper — as the relaxing energy moves up to your stomach and middle back. And as the muscles in your back relax, they sink softly and gently into the couch (or the surface on which you are reclining) — feeling safe, secure, and totally supported as the relaxing energy moves up to your chest and upper back....

And the relaxing energy moves across your shoulders, allowing them to sag and droop comfortably, and it begins to move down your arms, relaxing your upper arms, your elbows, your lower arms, your wrists, your hands, and even your fingers — deeply, comfortably relaxed....

Now see and feel the relaxing energy moving up to your neck, relaxing all the muscles of your neck and throat. Notice how your throat opens as your neck muscles relax. Even the muscles in the back of your tongue become deeply, comfortably relaxed....

Now see and feel the relaxing energy moving up to your face and head, relaxing first the muscles around your mouth and jaw. Notice how your teeth want to separate as your jaw muscles relax — becoming deeply, comfortably relaxed....

And now see and feel the relaxing energy moving up to relax the muscles around your nose, your cheeks, your eyes, your brow, and even your scalp....

All your muscles are becoming deeply, comfortably relaxed — more relaxed with each breath you breathe.

And with your next breath, imagine your energy body expanding, expanding out inch by inch, expanding out through the soles of your feet. Your conscious mind may not know how to expand your energy body, but your unconscious mind does. So let it take over now, easily and effortlessly expanding your energy body out through the soles of your feet....

Pause

And now bring your energy body back to normal, focusing on the difference between this state of expansion and your normal state of contraction....

Pause

And now imagine your energy body expanding out through

the top of your head, again expanding out inch by inch.... And, once, again, bring your energy body back to normal....

And now let your energy body blow up like a balloon, getting bigger and bigger, lighter and lighter, more and more expanded. Keep expanding your energy body, letting it fill the whole room, getting bigger and bigger, more and more expanded, lighter and lighter. It is so light that it floats up, through the ceiling, through the roof, and moves very swiftly in space back to the place where you now live....

Pause

Imagine yourself floating down in front of your front door. Reach out and touch that door and if it feels rough or smooth, warm or cool....

As you become aware of the temperature and texture of the door, describe the door— What color it is, what it's made of, what's above the door, below it, and to either side. Are there windows, lamps, plants, columns? Describe any distinguishing features—panes of glass, panels of wood, the color of the door handle....

Pause

And now float up to the roof of your house; look around in all directions; be aware of any sounds that you might hear; notice any sensations such as the temperature of the air, the breeze on your face, and the feeling of the roof itself under your feet. Describe whatever you are aware of....

Pause

Now float up even higher, until you are about a mile up, floating on a white, puffy cloud....

Is it daylight or night?

Make it [the other] and say aloud that you've done so....

Now change it back again....

Now, if it is daylight, leave it that way; if it is night, make it bright daylight....

And who is making it night and day? (Wait for answer.)

That's right. You are. In the same way that you have control over the lightness and the darkness, you also have the ability to move forward and backward in time. And, this place where you are, this white puffy cloud a mile up, is your contact point with your teacher, guides, and higher self, who you now ask to guide you back in time, back to a time, either in this life or another, that will help you understand (whatever issue, relationship, or condition that the you wish to understand).

And, as you float down, you float backward in time....

Pause

And, as your feet touch the ground once again, look down at your feet and describe the surface on which you are landing. Is it grass, sand, stone, wood, metal, water...? (Wait for answer.)

What are you wearing on your feet? Shoes, sandals, boots,

moccasins? Maybe you're barefoot. (Wait for answer.)

Now look at your legs and the rest of your body. What kind of clothing are you wearing? (Wait for answer.) Let yourself know how old you are. Just let an age pop into your mind, trusting the validity of that information, however it comes. (Wait for answer.) Are you a man/boy or a woman/girl? (Wait for answer.) You might even know your name. And, if you don't know, it might come to you later. (Wait for answer.)

And now, look around and notice, are there trees, buildings, mountains, animals, or other people? What is around you? (Wait for answer.) And, in the same way, let yourself know where you are, what country or part of the world. (Wait for answer.)

What are you feeling? (Wait for answer.)

Now, move forward or backward in time to a moment of emotional importance in that life, and describe where you are; what you are doing, what you are saying; who is with you; and what you see, hear, sense, and feel.

[At this point, I am guided by whatever the regressee brings forth. I am also channeling energy to the regressee throughout this process for mental and emotional clarity. If anything is unclear to them, I move them back up to the cloud a mile up, where they can contact their teachers and guides and obtain clarification. In that place, I tell them they are also free of emotional reaction.

We move through the life at this point, more or less sequentially, from emotional high point to emotional high point, culminating with his/her death.

At the point of death, I say:]

"Watch as your soul separates from your physical body. And in that state of perfected awareness, look back over that life and notice if there are any relationships or events that stand out as incomplete in any way. Perhaps you are still holding onto guilt or resentment over something someone said or did. Let those scenes or events come into your awareness, one by one. And, if you are ready to forgive that person now, including yourself, [and they usually are at this point] see them before you, and allow the forgiveness to flow from your heart to theirs. Notice what happens as you do." (Wait for answer. Repeat as necessary.)

Pause

Now ask your teachers and guides to let you know what your purpose was in that lifetime. What lessons did you come to learn and how did you learn them? Let that information come in whatever way it wants to come, as words, thoughts, images, or even symbols, trusting the validity of the information in whatever form it takes. (Wait for response.)

Pause

Now it's time to say goodbye to your teachers and guides. Now that you can contact them again, at any time, simply by closing your eyes, getting quiet, and floating back up to that puffy, white cloud a mile up. And, each time you do so, it becomes easier and easier to make contact.

Pause

As you begin to float down, move forward in time back into

this time, back into this space, back into this room, and back into your physical body. Taking all the time you need to bring your awareness fully back to the present, and when you are ready, open your eyes.

A certified hypnotherapist, Reiki Master, and discoverer of the Amanohuna system of healing, Arthur Cataldo co-directs the Center for Transformation on Sanibel Island, Florida with his wife, Anne, a channel for the Master Teacher, Simon. He conducts personal and intuitive development seminars nationally.

Male/Female

59

Contacting the Archetypal Female

Guide: Mary Ellen Carne, Ph.D.

"I use this meditation to help both women and men get in touch with and bring to consciousness essential feminine archetypal energy within themselves."

Introduction

From the beginning of time, wise women through the ages have worshiped the female creative force in the form of the Great Mother. The Great Mother, revered Creatress of life, the archetypal Female Principle, has many names: Sophia, Lilith, Nut, Isis, Ishtar, Inanna, Diana, Hecate, Artemis, Selene, Demeter, Astarte, Hathor, Aphrodite, Kali, Bellona, Harmonia, Shin Moo, Rhea, Luna, Cybele, Trivia, Cerridwen, Gaia.... For many centuries before written history, the female principle was the Moon Goddess, The Creatrix, Giver of Life, Giver of Wisdom, Queen of Heaven.

You will spend the next few minutes of clock time entering the place of knowing within yourselves in order to reconnect with your own knowing of the Female Principle. She has always been with us, but her full power has been hidden, buried, and veiled for many thousands of years. The Female Principle, the Goddess comes to women and men bringing whatever is necessary for healing rebirth. She appears in dreams, a vision, or through a spark of intuition or creativity, and serves as a catalyst to awaken energies that flow through and empower women's bodies and psyches.

The Journey

You are slowly moving now, through your breathing, to that place of knowing, the place within you that recognizes the Female Principle. Surround yourself with a cloud of warm, protective light, light of your own making which both nurtures and protects you. Find yourself relaxing more with each breath; your breath becoming slower and slower, moving lower and lower....

Become aware of the wind, hear a light rush and hum that tells you it is there. Feel the breeze sweep through your mind, clearing it of all thoughts, sweeping away all fears, all pain, all anger, all doubt. Let the strong, clean wind sweep over you and gently carry you deep into the recesses of your soul, deep into the recesses of your psyche, that ancient place of knowing....

Pause

Let the wind carry away your strain, your tension, your confusion and replace it with relaxation and receptivity. Notice how clean and clear you feel now, how very light and clear you feel, light enough to just float in a state of relaxation, protected, and enfolded in a circle of clarity and light....

Find yourself now moving gently and freely into a moonlit grotto, a beautiful cave that is covered with crystals so that your own clear light reflects within it. In this sacred and magical space, you will meet whoever or whatever represents the Female Principle to you. Allow an image of her to take form, taking whatever comes to you....

Pause

Now hear your representation of the Female Principle speak to you. "I am the Mother of All Living, and my love is poured out upon the earth. I am the beauty of the green earth and the white moon among the stars and the mystery of the waters and the desires in the heart of woman. Let yourself be reflected in me, knowing that I am within you and have been from the beginning. I am spirit, higher power, source of love, natural wisdom, the wisdom that knows without knowing how. I am the power of female knowing, instinctual and intuitive." Take a few moments to commune with this inner part of you, this ancient female wisdom. Ask her to tell you who she is and how she manifests in your life or anything else you wish to know from her. Receive her message in whatever form it takes....

Pause

Knowing that you have been in touch with the deepest and most ancient roots of womanhood and recognizing that you were in touch with a spiritual essence that is an integral part of your being, give yourself permission to reclaim the power of your own female being, the archetypal Feminine Principle and acknowledge what you have just received....

Pause

Do what you need to now, in preparation for leaving this sacred place. Know that you have called upon the Female Principle and have seen and felt her reflected within your own body. You have called upon the Female Principle whose energy, like a woman's energy flows with the cycles of the earth and the universe. You have called upon and recognized the Female Principle within you, the Female Principle whose circle is never broken, never lost, whose circle you are a part of wherever you go. With this knowledge, the feelings and the symbols your have received, gradually and caringly bring yourself back to the room... and in your own time... stretch and be fully present.

Mary Ellen Carne is a masseuse, a stress management consultant, and a teacher of the Feminine Principal in Madison, Wisconsin. She teaches in an experiential manner that includes guided imagery and the sharing of personal experience through art, music, movement, and group discussion.

60

Flower Focus

Guide: Mina Jo Sirovy, Ph.D.

"Spring, a jasmine bush, and a full moon inspired this meditation."

Introduction

I use this meditation with clients who need self-esteem heightened and with men who need to get in touch with their female energy. It promotes the awareness of one's need for tender loving care, helps one to have patience with the unfolding process, and encourages one to "touch" others. I recommend this imagery be practiced when you cannot get out in nature or when identification with a flower is appropriate.

The Journey

Breathe deeply as you sit quietly with eyes closed—relaxing and focusing inward on each breath. Realize that you are breathing in what the plants in the room are breathing out, and they are inhaling what you are exhaling. Know that you are one with all of nature, breathing in and out, sharing the same air.

Pause

As you are sitting in a peaceful repose, accept the gift of a beautiful flower into your folded hands. Allow the flower to be one of your own choosing and notice the details of its petals, its colors, its aroma. As it takes shape, attend to the way it has unfolded and how long the stem is. This flower represents you in all your glory. It has taken sunshine, rain, and tender loving care to produce its blossoms. Have patience with your unfolding and see the beauty, in this stage of your life. Know that the adversity (the rain) can be a blessing in terms of growth. Realize that love (the sun's warmth) has encouraged the blooming. As the caretaker of this flower, you owe it and yourself gentleness, respect for its beauty, and time to grow and expand. Appreciate the artwork of a Higher Creator who lavishes love on each flower and brings it to its own perfection just as He/She has done with you. Enjoy the effect this fragrant flower has on you. Compare it to a jasmine bush that stays in one space but spreads its aroma to places the flower never sees. So it is with you. The essence of you flows forth to others, and you know not how many you touch.

Pause

Breathe deeply the gentle power of this exquisite particle of nature; allow every cell to be permeated with its beauty and harmony and color. Identify with your flower and know that you, too, can bloom again and again. Remember some of the beloved persons in your life and see them as flowers. Take some time now to gather these flowers together to form a lovely bouquet.

Pause

And when you have named each significant person as a

flower, see yourself in the middle of the bouquet surrounded by love and beauty. When you are fulfilled with the essence of your floral bouquet, allow yourself to come gracefully and gradually back to life on this physical plane where you can share your own glorious nature with those you meet.

Dr. Mina Sirovy, who resides in Oceanside, California, is a marriage, child, family therapist with degrees in psychology from the University of California; a master's degree from United States International University; and a Ph.D. from The Professional School for Psychological Studies, where she was also a professor. Dr. Sirovy is a transpersonal psychotherapist who calls herself a "stretch" instead of a "shrink."

61

Relationship Release

Guide: Lisa Zimmer

"To progress spiritually, it is important to resolve pending issues with other people."

Introduction

If you have unresolved issues from past relationships, you may seek to resolve these in order to enhance your spiritual growth. Such a release allows you to let go and progress and perhaps even notice visible changes in existing relationships.

The Journey

Begin by sitting, reclining, or lying in a comfortable position. Take a deep cleansing breath through your nose and exhale all anxiety and tension out of your mouth. Allow your breathing to regulate and release tension as you become relaxed.

Find yourself on a soft, sandy white beach at sunset, walking along the shore. You are alone, except for a person far ahead of you, who is walking toward you....

As the person gets closer you realize that it is someone you have an unsettled issue or problem with.

Pause

The person is now two feet in front of you.

You look into his or her eyes and you hold hands. As you grasp hands, you tell the person that you love him unconditionally.

Pause

As you look deeper into his eyes, you sense his feelings and emotions....

You feel the compassion and love overwhelm you as you wish this person well in his journey.... You embrace this person as you feel the compassion and love overwhelming you both. The energy of love allows you to release this person as you wish him well on his way.

You are feeling a sense of accomplishment by resolving unsettled issues with this person as you continue on your walk along the shore. You are very aware of the warmth of the sun, the sound of the waves crashing to shore, and the birds flying overhead. All feels peaceful in your environment.

Open your eyes at will.

Lisa Zimmer is a metaphysical consultant in Naples, Florida. She teaches classes on developing intuition and creative visualization.

I thank Divine Energy.

I thank the people who have been instrumental in physically helping to formulate all three meditation books.

I thank everyone who will use the meditations for personal and global growth.

In other words, I thank…

ONE IN ALL